EMMA AND CO.

EMMA AND CO.

by

SHEILA HOCKEN

LONDON
VICTOR GOLLANCZ LTD
1983

First Published May 1983
Second Impression May 1983

Published by arrangement with
Sphere Books Ltd

British Library Cataloguing in Publication Data
Hocken, Sheila
  Emma and co.
  1. Blind—Rehabilitation   2. Blindness—
  Psychological aspects
  I. Title
  362.4′1′0924   HV1598

ISBN 0-575-03252-9

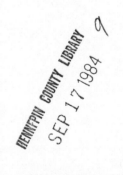

Printed in Great Britain at
The Camelot Press Ltd, Southampton

To
my mum, dad and brother Graham

ILLUSTRATIONS

Following page 44

Don, Sheila and Kerensa with Bracken and Ming
(*Leicester Mercury*)

Shadow, Teak, Buttons, Bracken and Mocha
(*Roger Willgoose*)

Bracken answering the telephone (*Rex Features*)

Following page 76

Bracken leading Emma (*Photographers International*)

At the Pro-Dogs Award: Bracken receives the medal for
Devotion to Duty on Emma's behalf from Leslie Scott
Ordish (*Pro-Dogs*)

Sheila and Bracken with Barbara Woodhouse and the other
medal winners

Emma and Bracken wearing their medals (*Rex Features*)

Following page 108

Kerensa and Mocha

Shadow (*Robin Bidgood*)

Shadow and Sheila doing an obedience test

Shadow and Teak

The puppy that went to be trained as a guide-dog
(*by permission of the Guide Dogs for the Blind Association*)

*Any photographs not individually credited were taken by Sheila and
Don Hocken.*

7

FOREWORD

I STILL CAN'T help feeling that I am the luckiest person in the world. So many wonderful things have happened to me in my thirty-odd years on this earth. Most people, I am sure, would think I'd been very unlucky in my lifetime. I was born into a virtually blind family. Both my parents had little sight. My brother, too, couldn't see much and I suffered from the same eye defect – hereditary cataracts – which, of course, caused retina damage. We weren't over-endowed with money either, but it's not money or sight that makes a life, it's the people around you. I was lucky enough to have parents who understood what it was like to be visually handicapped and were determined that my life would be as normal as possible. My father had been away to a school for the blind. My mother had spent her life from the age of ten on, when she lost her parents, in a children's home. So family life, to them, was of paramount importance and they were both determined that neither I nor Graham, my brother, would be sent away to a special school. So I attended the local junior school, Bluebell Hill, and went on to a secondary girls' school. There were lots of hardships, I don't deny that, but, again, I think I was lucky to be faced with those as a child. I learnt how to cope with everyday things. I was able to ignore the children who called me names like 'Bozz-Eyed' as I made my way to school. I never bothered if I walked into a lamp-post or fell over things that were left on the pavement. It was just normal to me. I couldn't read the blackboard, of course, but either someone sitting next to me, or the teacher, would help me and I got by. Admittedly, I wasn't terribly well educated. There was a lot I missed out on at school. But it taught me to make the best of what I had.

I left school in 1961 and was able to do a job as a telephonist. By that time the bit of sight that I had was going gradually, and I had to learn Braille. Life as a teenager, I am sure, is traumatic for most people. For me it certainly was. I was now having to cope with the realities of earning a living and getting to and from work. My social life became almost non-existent. I had to rely on friends and acquaintances to take me out, to go to dances, etc., but it was very difficult to fit in with a crowd of sighted teenagers. I'd get left behind, literally, walking along the pavement. I became more and more afraid of going out and meeting new people, so it was much easier to stop in at nights. I dread to think what would have happened to me if I hadn't heard about the Guide-Dogs for the Blind Association, and met Emma.

The social worker for the blind advised me to apply for a guide-dog. My application was accepted and I went for my month's training at the Leamington Spa Guide-Dog Training Centre in July 1966, and there I was given Emma – a small, chocolate brown, thick coated Labrador. Even in the first few months of our partnership Emma helped me tremendously and changed my life. What I didn't realise then was how much she was going to give me during the following years. Every guide-dog owner I've ever met states categorically that they have the best guide-dog that was ever trained. There are thousands of blind people in Britain today who rely completely on their dogs to take them to work, to take them out to do the shopping, and to help them lead as normal a social life as possible. Being blind is a terrible handicap, for Man, above all creatures, is a very visual animal. But nearly every blind person I've ever met, especially those with guide-dogs, accept their lot and make the best of it, and try to pretend that outside there isn't a visual world at all. It makes the struggle for equality a lot easier that way and, with the aid of a guide-dog, every blind person has mobility.

My first year with Emma as my guide-dog was full of exciting discoveries, the main one being that I was safe with her: she would take me through the busy streets of Nottingham to find the place where I worked; she would find bus stops for me, and when we got on the bus she'd find me an empty seat; she learnt the names of all the shops I needed to go to; she would find a letter-box or telephone box on request and she always remembered that a zebra crossing was by far the safest place to cross a road. Not only did I discover freedom, I made lots of friends and had a social life at last. Because I had Emma, I could go to evening classes, and I did courses in the Writer's Craft (short story writing, etc.), Make-up and Beauty, and Dressmaking. One of the many friends I made was Anita, whom I met at the Writer's Class, and we shared a flat together for two years. I needed my independence. I needed to be like other girls of my age, and sharing a flat was a step in the right direction. And then I met Don, my husband-to-be, actually over the telephone, through another blind friend of mine, George Miller.

I had met George originally through Radio Nottingham. He ran a programme especially for blind people and I had done quite a few programmes for him – about guide-dogs, of course. Don and I fell in love immediately but it was quite a few years before we were able to settle down and get married, for Don had a broken marriage to sort out. But what would I have done without Emma? Emma was the one who always took me out to meet Don, who I felt secure with. I didn't have to rely on other people, for Emma was always reliable, always keen to go wherever I wanted. As if that wasn't enough luck in my life – meeting Emma and then Don – I was to have something else wonderful happen to me.

I had, of course, been to many eye specialists in the past and, as children, both my brother and I had eye operations, but none of them had worked, until Graham and I heard of a Mr Shearing who was perfecting a new type of operation to remove congenital cataracts. Although Mr Shearing had offered to try to help me get a little bit of sight, he was very dubious and suggested that even if he did the operation and it was successful, I would still need a guide-dog. But I decided to have the operation. Anything was better than nothing, and I went into hospital in September 1975. And I came out, ten days later, with sight, to a new and beautiful, colourful world. That happened seven years ago, and I wrote about it in my first book *Emma and I*, but I still thrill at the sight I have. To wake up in the morning and to see the sun shining. To see the rain glistening on the leaves. To look forward with excitement to watching the snow fall in winter and the daffodils coming up in spring, and I am always out in the garden when it rains and there is a touch of sunshine, just in the hope of seeing a rainbow.

And then, as I related in my second book *Emma V.I.P.*, Don and I were blessed with a baby daughter, Kerensa. We both knew that there was a 50–50 chance that she would be blind, but after much thought and discussion we decided to take that chance and, again, we were very lucky. Kerensa has perfect sight. So you see why I feel I am one of the most fortunate people in the world – to have had so much in so little time! And it was Emma who gave me all this: she opened the door to freedom. I have always loved dogs. In fact, one of my earliest memories, as a child, is of me wanting to go and stroke every dog and my mother warning me not to and trying to pull me away in case they bit. But she never changed my affection for those lovely creatures, and Emma cemented that bond forever. I am sometimes afraid of how much I respect and love all the dogs around me. I could never live without one close by me. For almost ten years I relied solely upon Emma, not only for my eyes but as a very close friend. Emma has retired now. She retired at the age of eleven, after my successful operation, and it's my pleasure to take her for a walk, to see her running about the fields and enjoying herself and, whatever happens to us both in the future, there will always be a part of Emma inside me.

EMMA AND CO.

CHAPTER ONE

IT WAS CHRISTMAS Eve. Don, Kerensa, myself and, of course, Emma had gone to visit my parents. It was a ritual: we always went there for tea on Christmas Eve. Kerensa was just two and beginning to take an interest in what was happening around her. It was very exciting, not only for her but for me as well. Seeing her face light up with excitement at Christmas trees and pointing out the pictures of Santa Claus, I was reliving my childhood Christmasses – but this time with my sight. Then half-way through tea, I suddenly remembered I'd left the pan of dog meat on the stove.

'Oh no!' I groaned aloud and dropped my knife and fork. I looked across at Don.

'What's the matter, petal?'

'I think I've left the dog meat pan on. Oh dear, what are we going to do?'

It wouldn't have been so bad if Bracken and Buttons hadn't been shut in the kitchen at home. They were our two new dogs. Buttons had joined us in the September and Bracken, who had been a birthday present to me from Don, in the October. Buttons was just over a year old and Bracken was coming up for three months. We'd decided not to take them on our usual Christmas Eve visit. Mum and Dad quite like dogs, but they aren't that keen.

'Are you sure you've left it on?' Don asked me.

'Pretty sure.' I panicked instantly. I had visions of the house being on fire and Bracken and Buttons being burnt to death. Thank God we hadn't left Emma, I thought.

'I'd better go back and have a look.' Don, always cool, calm and practical.

'I'll come with you.' I got up before he could say no and put my coat on.

'No, petal. You stop here. What about Kerensa? Stay and keep her occupied. You can't leave her with your Mum and Dad.'

'But I must come. Something might have happened to the dogs.'

'No, no. You stop here. I can get there just as fast without you.'

'Well, ring me when you get back, and hurry up.'

'I will, I will. Now don't panic. We haven't been gone that long. It should be all right.'

As soon as Don had closed the front door behind him I began to panic even more. I could imagine the house on fire and I could see hordes of fire-engines streaming down Nottingham Road, Stapleford. Oh, Bracken and Buttons . . . please God that they were all right. I went back into the dining room where Mum and Dad and my brother, Graham, were still eating tea. Poor Mum, being deaf, hadn't heard what had happened and, as far as she was concerned, Don had just put his knife and fork down in the middle of his tea and gone.

'What's the matter with him?' she asked as she came over to me. I explained. 'Thank goodness for that,' she said. 'I thought you'd had a row and he'd walked out and left you.'

That made me laugh, even in the middle of my panic. Don and I having a row? That was unheard of! 'What am I going to do?' I kept saying to Mum. 'I wish I'd gone with him. I know – I'll ring Betty.' Betty was one of those friends you can always rely on. She lives round the corner from us and no matter what the crisis . . . ring Betty!

'Betty, it's me. I'm at my Mum's. I think I've left a pan of meat on at home . . . you could probably get round quicker than Don, he's just left.'

'Where's the key?' Betty asked.

'There isn't one!'

'Well, how am I going to get in then?'

'You can't,' I said.

'What's the point of me going then?'

'At least you can see if the place is on fire,'' I said, 'and if it is full of smoke, break the window and let Bracken and Buttons out. Oh, Betty, please go. It won't take you long.'

'All right, all right. Don't worry.'

'If you see Don, tell him to ring me, won't you?'

'Yes, I will. Don't worry, I'll go straight away.'

Mum sat watching the television. Dad sat in the chair thinking, as usual . . . of things like the next song he was going to compose. Graham, my brother, was keeping Kerensa entertained on the carpet with a little doll he had bought her for Christmas. Emma, unconcerned as usual, was curled up in front of the gas fire. But I couldn't sit still. I had to pace the floor, fingers crossed, brain trying to block out what might have happened to Bracken and Buttons. I have always had a phobia about losing a chiid or a dog in a fire and I was beginning to believe it had been a foresight. Then after what seemed an age, the phone rang. It was Don.

'Oh, thank goodness! Have you saved them?'

'Yes, I've saved them. You hadn't left the pan of meat on.'

'Oh dear!' I was glad I hadn't, of course, but I felt rather stupid having insisted Don left his tea and dashed home. I had burnt a hole in three dog meat pans in the last month. I was thinking of turning professional. 'They're all right then?'

'Yes, they're fine, but you should see the state of the kitchen.'

'Why, what's the matter with it?'

'You know that nice new Cushionfloor Vinolay we had put down the other week?'

'Yes,' I said.

'Most of it's not there any more. Bracken's torn it up and eaten it.'

'How could he have done that?'

'And that's not all,' Don interrupted. 'He's eaten a hole in the split-level cooker.'

'A *hole*! What do you mean?'

'You'll see it when you get home. There's a great big hole chewed in the side.'

'What are you going to do?' I asked him.

'What do you mean, what am I going to do? There's not a

lot I can do. I'll try and stick a bit of the floor back down. We'll have to see if we can get some more pieces. What I'd like to do to Bracken isn't repeatable over the telephone.'

I could well understand what he meant, but how could that little innocent puppy do so much damage? I wondered. We knew it wasn't Buttons. She had been a chewer, but not for very long and she was over a year old now. She had grown out of that habit. Labradors, I hate to admit, do tend to be very destructive. Not all of them, just some, but then I suppose some of every breed are destructive, so I mustn't condemn Labradors. But if I were to tell you what Bracken has eaten, chewed up and ruined it would take the whole of this book, so I won't bother. Luckily for us, we only have one Bracken. Buttons had chewed, as I mentioned. Only once, but a very important once.

I had done a lot of television programmes about the book, *Emma and I*. Emma had gone with me and we'd had lots of fun and met some really nice people, but there was just one programme I really wanted to be on, one that I enjoyed watching every week, and that was the Michael Parkinson chat show. There wasn't a hope in hell's chance of me getting on there. I mean, they only have famous people on – film stars and the like – but secretly, I hoped. My publishers told me they'd sent the book to the programme to see if there was any chance of my getting an interview and, by a sheer fluke, it came off. They weren't interested at first. They said they had plenty of material like my book and a big star was coming from America (I can't remember who it was now) but then I saw a rainbow. You might think this very silly, but I have great faith in rainbows. After the operation on my eyes one of the things I desperately wanted to see was a rainbow. I'd heard so much about them and they sounded so beautiful. It was six months before I saw one and it was marvellous, impressive, stirring, romantic, and every time I see a rainbow something really lovely happens to me. So I am always on the look-out for them. And I saw a rainbow in Leicester. Not a real one, but a pub called The Rainbow. It had the same effect. I knew something marvellous was going to happen, I just didn't know what. Then that very evening I had a message from the publishers to say that we had been accepted for the Parkinson Show, as the American film star had let them down. Could I go down on Saturday? I could. I was only left with three days to worry and think about it. They were going to send a taxi – a big one they assured me, because of Emma. Emma was coming up for fourteen years old and her comfort was uppermost. If I wanted to go anywhere with her, I had to make sure that she was going to be happy and comfortable. She had always been very adept at curling up into tight spots as a young dog but now she became stiff unless there was plenty of room for her to stretch out, and that meant a decent car for her to travel down in.

'Yes,' they kept saying, 'we'll send a nice big taxi for you.'

'Lovely.' And I said to Don, 'Perhaps there'll be enough room for somebody to come with us.' A big taxi to me and him meant a big taxi. The sort of Daimler-type that can seat three or four, even five, in the back and still have plenty of room.

'What about asking Deirdre?'

'Yes, that would be nice,' I said. Deirdre was John's wife. John is Don's partner in his chiropody practice. John had been to America with us and we had asked Deirdre if we had anywhere exciting to go, television-wise, would she like to come? It's amazing how you get used to this sort of thing. The inside of a television studio is old hat to me now but I remember when it was a very exciting happening, and friends always want to see what they're like, to see what's on the other side of the camera.

'What about Sylvia and Mick as well?' Don asked. 'There would be plenty of room, wouldn't there?'

'Yes, of course.' Mick was Don's brother, Sylvia his wife.

'I'll get on the phone to them right away,' he said.

I could see it was going to be a right old outing. Mick, Sylvia and Deirdre were all absolutely delighted. Just like me, though, Sylvia and Deirdre were in a panic about having hair-dos, and getting dresses for the evening.

'What are you wearing?' Sylvia rang me back to ask.

'I don't know yet, haven't really thought. I'll go and have a look in the wardrobe. If there's nothing suitable, I suppose I'll have to go down to the shops.'

'Mm, I don't know what to wear. Do you think it'll be warm?'

'I think so,' I said. 'It usually is in television studios. In fact, it's boiling hot with all those lights.'

'I've got a nice summer dress. Anyway, let me know what colour you're wearing first, will you?'

'Yes, fine, Sylvia.'

I looked in the wardrobe. There was nothing I really fancied wearing for the Parkinson Show. After all, it had to be something extra special. I was lucky though – I saw something really nice in one of the local shops: a velvet suit in wine colour. I'm crackers about velvet, probably because it feels so good. Touch is still an all-important sense to me. Not only must a thing look good, it must feel good. I would have preferred green but wine is my second favourite colour. I love green because of the grass and the trees. There are so many different shades of green, I never cease to be surprised at them. The spring and the summer, even the autumn, turn up different shades of green and there's always a different shade when snow has been down. That was one of my big surprises. The grass stays there underneath the snow. Anyway, I settled for the wine-coloured velvet suit, which meant that I had to buy new shoes. I decided to buy black patent ones because they'd match everything.

Saturday came and we were all waiting for this lovely big taxi they had promised to send us. Don and I, Deirdre, Mick and Sylvia and Emma. When the taxi man arrived, we rushed out with great excitement. It was almost like emigrating, let alone doing a television programme. When I saw the car that stood at the bottom of our drive, I was horrified. I looked around to make sure there were no other cars standing nearby, but when the driver opened the door, I realized that it must be the one. It looked more like a heap on wheels to me, something that Mr Ford had invented back in the 1910s. It was incredibly old, incredibly battered and incredibly dirty. We had to put newspaper down in it before we dared to sit down and as for room, well, I stood there on the pavement trying to work out how we could all get in. I was completely unable to accept the fact that it was impossible. All I could hear was the Michael Parkinson theme tune and him standing there saying I hadn't arrived. As no one else seemed to be doing anything, I took charge.

'Right, Deirdre, Sylvia and Mick in the back.' I think they were so shocked, they didn't protest. They all squeezed in the back. I had a job shutting the door.

'Emma, you get in the front. Oh no, no. That won't work, I'll sit in the front.' I got in the passenger seat. Emma, by this time, had climbed over into the driver's seat. I looked round to see Mick, Sylvia and Deirdre settled in the back, a little bit like sardines in a tin but, nevertheless, they were in. Then I noticed the driver. He was leaning on the bonnet of the car gazing into the distance, with a Park Drive hanging out of the corner of his mouth. Don tapped on the window.

'Petal, the driver's not in, let alone me.'

'Oh no,' I groaned. 'It just won't work.' I got out of the car and, undaunted, tried again. 'Right, I think you'd better get in first,' I said to the driver. He walked casually round to the driver's side and sat in behind the wheel as if we had all day. 'You get in the back, Emma. Right, I'll sit in with you. That's better, we've plenty of room.' But there were still four people to get in one front passenger seat. I climbed out on to the pavement again. 'It won't work,' I said to Don. 'It just won't work. What are we going to do?'

Then Mick stepped in. 'Of course it'll work,' he said. 'I'll take my car. Me and Sylvia and Deirdre can travel down in our car. That will leave you plenty of room.'

I saw the look of sheer relief on Deirdre's face. Without any argument she went straight back to their car. It was all right for those three. Poor me, Don and Emma had to be rattled and bashed and skidded all the way down the M1 to London. It was a terrible experience, and one I don't wish to repeat in a hurry. Now, if I ever get asked down to television shows, my first question is what sort of transport will there be? – and I mean a detailed account. I won't settle for, 'Oh, it'll be okay, there'll be plenty of room.'

It wasn't until we were about half-way down the M1 that I began to notice something strange about one of my feet. It didn't seem to be very comfortable any more, so I had a feel. I was stricken with horror to find out that one of my shoes had been half chewed away. The heel had gone out completely. Instead of being normal shoes, I'd got one sling back and one ordinary. I couldn't believe it. I took it off my foot to examine it.

'Don!' I said. 'Look at this shoe!'

'Good grief, what's happened to it?'

'It looks as if somebody's chewed it,' I said.

'Who? There's only Emma in the car and she's been fast asleep.'

'It must have happened before I put it on.' I couldn't imagine how I could possibly have put a half-chewed shoe on without realizing it.

'You must have noticed,' Don said, as if he was reading my thoughts.

'Yes, I would have thought so. I was probably so excited and in a hurry, I just didn't. I just slung them on my feet and hoped for the best.'

'What are you going to do? You can't go on the Parkinson Show with a half-chewed shoe, can you now?' he said.

'There's only one thing for it,' I said. 'We'll have to find a shoe shop.'

He made a pretence of looking out of the window on the M1. 'Can't see any round here,' he said with a smile.

'No, you wouldn't, would you? But there's bound to be one somewhere when we get off the motorway.'

'I don't think we're going on a shopping route.' He leaned over and asked the driver. 'When we get off the M1, do you think you could find a shoe shop?'

'A shoe shop!' he retorted. I think he thought he was hearing things.

'Yes, that's right. We want a shoe shop desperately.'

'Oh, a shoe shop. Well, I'll have a look.'

We took an earlier exit off the motorway. We knew Mick and Sylvia following us would be rather surprised, but they followed us. We kept looking round and seeing Mick mouthing things like, 'This isn't the way to the BBC,' and waving his hands furiously. It was very difficult for him to understand our signs through the back window. It was so dirty we could barely see out. So they just had to be patient until we stopped outside a shoe shop. Mick, Sylvia and Deirdre immediately rushed out of the car and over to us.

'What's the matter?' Mick said. 'What's happened, is there something wrong?'

Instead of explaining, I picked my shoe up and showed it him. He looked at the shoe and then down at Emma.

'Good heavens, did she do that?'

'No, of course she didn't. It could only have been Buttons. She must have sneaked upstairs while we were having lunch and found it in my bedroom.'

'It would have been cheaper to give her some of your lunch,' Mick said, laughing.

I wasn't in the mood to see the funny side at the time, especially as the shoe shop turned out to be quite an expensive one.

I was pleasantly surprised when we arrived at the television studios with plenty of time to spare and still in one piece. It was awe-inspiring to discover that I was to appear with Peter Alliss, the professional golfer, and Johnny Mathis, the brilliant American singer. Emma, as always, was oblivious to the importance of Michael Parkinson and she confidently led the way down those terrible steps. Everybody dreads those stairs on chat shows – I wonder why they have them? As Michael Parkinson began to ask me the questions, Emma started to snore.

'Do you mean to tell me that that dog,' he said, pointing to the chocolate form at my feet, 'actually knew what a post office meant?'

As if in answer, Emma got up, looked at him, gave one of those snorts that she's famous for, turned her back on him and went to sleep. If Michael himself didn't take that as an answer, the audience certainly did.

CHAPTER TWO

BOOKS, TELEVISION PROGRAMMES, visits to radio stations, children, dogs and cats – my life seemed to be so hectic I hardly knew where I was going or what I was doing. And then there was the other side of it, the horrible side. I suddenly discovered that I was self-employed and I'd got to do something about it. There was no Pay-As-You-Earn where tax had already been taken from my wage packet. How simple it had been when I was a telephonist! Now it was up to me to sort it all out. Well, I couldn't. It's as simple as that. I haven't the brain for that sort of thing. So Don and I decided that we would employ an accountant. I had heard that there was a nice friendly one down in Stapleford so I rang him up one day and asked if it would be possible for him to come and see me.

'I've got a young baby,' I explained, 'and no one to look after her at the moment.'

'Yes, that's fine. I can pop down tomorrow afternoon if you like. It'll only take about an hour to sort out what you need doing.'

Mr Summers duly arrived. Since I've been able to see, I've found that gradually I'm falling into the trap of all sighted people – judging on first sight, as it were. As a blind person I could never do this. I would go on voice, of course, but I found I usually waited till the real character, the real inside person, came out. I look at someone and instantly form a judgement (I might add that it's often completely wrong), but I've found I'm going further than that and categorizing people. You know the sort of thing: I imagine all lorry drivers are big, burly fellows with curly hair. And I had a very clear picture of how I expected my accountant to look: very small, thin, balding on top, steel-rimmed spectacles and a long parrot-like nose. So, you can imagine my surprise when the man I opened the door to was tall, very well-built, had dark wavy hair and a moustache. To be honest, he looked more like a gun-slinger than an accountant. 'Mr Summers?' I asked rather tentatively.

'Yes, how do you do. Call me Ray.' He gave my hand a firm shake, walked into the lounge and made himself at home on the settee. 'Right then, shall we start at the beginning?' he said in a lovely Nottinghamshire accent. 'Can I have a look at your books?'

'Erm . . . books. Erm . . . you mean . . . book. You'd like to have a look at the book.' I picked a copy of *Emma and I* off the shelf and handed it to him. He hadn't read it then. I am one of those writers who always assumes no one has read their books and if I ever get stopped in the street or receive letters saying that people have, I still can't help being surprised. It's marvellous that they've actually chosen my book out of all those hundreds on sale in the bookshop. Mr Summers didn't take the book from me but looked at me strangely.

'No, no, books. You know. Where you keep all your earnings, receipts and expenditure.'

'Oh, *books*!' I said. 'I haven't got any.' I thought I'd better be quite honest and open with him from the start.

'Do you mean you haven't kept any?' he said.

I saw total horror written all over his face and I knew he had the urge to pick up his briefcase and run. 'Er . . . no,' I said. 'I don't know how to. That's why I rang you.'

'Well, how do you know what you've earned? How do you know what you've spent? What about tax?'

'Er . . . yes,' I said. 'I have a rough idea.'

'A rough idea's no good.' He began to mop his brow with a handkerchief.

'I'm sure I can find out,' I assured him, trying to stop him leaving. 'Would you like a cup of tea?'

'Yes, I think I'd better.'

I was just beginning to reassure him that I could find out what I'd earned and more or less had an idea of what I'd spent when Hera came in. Hera is one of my Siamese cats – a

25

very beautiful Long Sveldt Redpoint, a champion in fact. She walked round the lounge carrying her tail high in the air, giving little purring noises. Siamese cats tend to be a little bit like Labradors and perhaps that's why I'm very fond of them both. They are very dog-like creatures. They're also terrible scavengers. Unbeknown to me, Hera had been on the scavenge. Now don't get me wrong. Siamese don't have delicate stomachs, but then I'm sure something would be wrong with my stomach if I'd eaten two used tea bags, a polythene wrapper, half a fish paper and a few tin-foil milk bottle tops. Well, I guessed that's what she'd eaten. . . . She decided to sit on the settee next to Mr Summers. I wouldn't say he disliked animals – before he came to visit me – but he wasn't very fond of Siamese cats, especially when one kept trying to poke papers out of his briefcase. I could see he was gradually sliding a little bit further up the settee when, suddenly, Hera sat bolt upright and was terribly sick all over him. I've never seen such a big man move so fast. With one leap he was off the settee and at the other side of the room, standing there with his hands in the air, looking down at his suit, not quite knowing what to do. I had to sponge him down with very strong smelling disinfectant and promise to put the cat out, before he'd continue with the paperwork.

Needless to say, Mr Summers declined to visit me again, especially when he heard I'd acquired two more Labradors – Buttons and Bracken. Big dogs don't like me, he informed me, and would I mind going to see him? I could understand it, especially when Bracken was a puppy because anything that didn't move out of the way quickly enough was chewed. I seem to be painting a very black – or should I say chocolate brown? – picture of Bracken, but really it's not true. He has been very wicked in his time but he's also done lots of really lovely things and I certainly wouldn't have been without him. I think (not including Emma, of course, because I really do never include Emma when I talk about dogs) Bracken is probably the most intelligent dog I've ever met and certainly the most expressive. He can change his face from looking totally miserable to grinning all over in half a second. One of his best expressions, though, is his guilty look. He seems to look at me from hooded eyes and ears placed back. I call this his Rose Petal Look because his ears curl round like rose petals. It was an expression I saw a lot of, especially when Kerensa was a toddler. It's amazing how one toddler and two chocolate Labradors can conspire to do so much damage between them, and Bracken would be the ring-leader. I was sitting in the lounge one day, thinking that Kerensa was happily playing in the kitchen, when Bracken came strolling in with that rose petal expression. 'Who me? No, never!' His face spoke volumes. I knew something had happened. I ran into the kitchen as fast as I could, to see the fridge totally empty, plastic bowls and empty packets littering the kitchen floor, Kerensa giggling happily away and Buttons finishing off the last half-pound of best butter. Bracken, by the expression on his face, had obviously thoroughly enjoyed the pound of lamb chops, bowl of Angel Delight, two pounds of lard and half a pound of sausages. Who do you blame in a situation like that? Kerensa for opening the fridge door? The dogs inciting her to do it, or eating what she gave to them? The only thing was to sit and have a good laugh about it. I was always amazed at a two-year-old having such ingenuity when it came to getting what she wanted out of the dogs. She couldn't reach the kitchen work surfaces or the drawers where the knives and forks were kept, but she could if she made Buttons lie on the floor so she could climb on top of her. And that's what I'd find her doing: a large wooden spoon in her hand, two pounds of sugar and a packet of soap powder mixed evenly along the work tops, the floor and all over Buttons' coat. Still, I have got used to living in this sort of total chaos and it doesn't worry me any more.

Kerensa loves animals. It's a good job or she'd have probably been the first two-year-old ever to run away from home. She always wants to be involved with the cats and dogs, asking to help feed them, or brush them, or train them. I have tried to involve Kerensa with the animals, to let her help me, because it makes her feel needed. She's an only child and having all those dogs about her might tend to make her think she's one too. In fact, it probably did when she was younger. I'd let her help me carry the food bowls down to the cats – until I discovered that she was pinching great lumps of Whiskas and raw liver before the cats ate it. And there was a point when no dog bowl with water in could be left down on the floor because Kerensa would be found on all fours licking out of it. Despite all this, Kerensa is the healthiest little girl I have ever seen. And as for helping to train the dogs, well that nearly created even more problems. But we solved it when we found a stuffed dog on wheels. His name is Bicky; he looks a bit like a yellow Labrador and is guaranteed never to run off.

'Mummy, I want a proper collar and lead for Bicky,' Kerensa announced one day as Don and I were in the kitchen having a cup of tea.

'Oh, yes. What for?'

'To train him, of course,' she said indignantly.

I handed her a piece of string out of the kitchen drawer.

'No, no!' she shrieked. 'I don't want that. I want a proper collar and lead!'

She settled for nothing less than a choke chain, put on the correct way, and a long training lead. Don and I watched as she led Bicky into the garden. She stood him on her left-hand side, took the lead in her right hand and said, 'Heel, Bicky.' She marched up the garden saying, 'Good dog. Heel. Come here, Bicky. You bad dog. Sit!' (Bicky, needless to say, ignored this command.) 'Stay!' she boomed up the garden. Still holding the lead, she walked away from him, turned and stood to face her stuffed dog on wheels. 'Bicky . . . come!' She gave such a violent jerk to the lead that Bicky rolled up the garden at about twenty miles-an-hour and bowled her over. She picked herself up off the floor and smacked him. 'You bad dog!' she said. After giving him a thorough going over she came into the kitchen.

'Daddy, Bicky won't sit down.'

Don looked at me as if to find a suitably convincing answer. Then inspiration struck. 'He's a bit stiff in his back legs,' he said. 'He's getting on, you know. He might not like to sit down. Just let him stand up when you do the stays, will you?'

'Mm, yes, all right then, I suppose I'll have to.' Off she marched to do some more heel work. I was beginning to think that Barbara Woodhouse had nothing on Kerensa's thunderous commands.

CHAPTER THREE

WHENEVER DON AND I get an invitation to go up to Yorkshire, we accept. Not only is it beautiful to look at, but the people are so warm and friendly. I think I must have some Yorkshire blood in me because I always feel at home there. If I were going to leave Nottinghamshire, then it would only be for Yorkshire. So when I received an invitation to appear on a chat show in Yorkshire, of course I accepted.

'Oh great!' Don said, when he saw the invitation. 'We could meet Harold and Betty up there. It's quite near them. Haven't you a book signing in Hull?'

'Yes, that's right,' I told him. 'They can show us where the book shop is.'

Harold and Betty live in a little village called Brough, just outside Hull.

'I'll give them a ring and see if they'll meet us up there.'

It was arranged that Harold and Betty would meet us in Hull. We'd do the television programme first and then go on to the book signing. Emma, by this time, was far too old to be dragged about in cars and in and out of television and radio studios, so Bracken was voted as her understudy. A good job he made of it too . . . most of the time. Getting Kerensa a baby-sitter also meant getting a dog-sitter for Emma so that Don and I and Bracken could go off up into Yorkshire. The television show was live, with an audience. I like doing chat shows with an audience because a camera is so cold to work to. If you think you've made a joke the camera won't laugh, but I can tell from the reaction of an audience whether it was funny or not.

We had a cosy little set in front of the audience: a round settee and table with a bowl of flowers (the microphone was hidden in the flowers) on a beautiful sheepskin rug, which really set the scene. I was to walk on with Bracken and sit down next to the interviewer, Shelley Rhodes. I'd met her years before when she'd worked for a newspaper and had come down to see me after my operation to write a piece about my miracle, so I felt even more at home than ever. Bracken was going to enjoy himself, I could tell that from the look on his face as soon as I sat down next to Shelley. He surveyed the audience carefully and weighed the cameras up. He gets an expression in his eyes that I know means: This could be a terrible bore, but don't worry I'll think of something. It's fascinating to me to be able to look into eyes and see expressions and different colours. I never realized how eyes and their expression and colour could give a character to someone's face, either human or dog. I can often judge a dog's temperament just by looking at its eyes, especially the colour. Emma has very dark, brown, soft, trusting eyes. Bracken has eyes the colour of a ripe pear. Buttons, who, in my opinion, is rather uncharacteristic of a Labrador, has cold, gold eyes. In a dog, that always denotes to me that it can be quite nasty, not to be trusted, probably scheming. All those things Buttons can lay claim to. Of course, she's perfectly all right with the family, particularly Kerensa, but when strangers are about, you can't trust her.

'You haven't brought Emma with you,' Shelley began the interview. 'This is Bracken, is it?'

Bracken looked at her, put his ears back in that rose petal expression of his and grinned. We tried to get on with the interview but Bracken had spotted the microphone hidden in a flower. He pushed his nose in and began to rootle into the flower bowl. I could imagine the sort of snuffling, banging noises that everyone was hearing and tried to drag him out without looking as if I was using force, which was a bit difficult because Bracken is rather heavy. I could see a man wearing headphones at the other end of the studio jumping up and down waving his arms.

'And then what happened?' Shelley asked me.

Then what happened? I thought. What have I just said? Goodness me, I had to think hard. It was difficult to concentrate on answering questions, and on a camera, an audience and Bracken. At long last, I managed to get him away from the flower vase, a few yellow petals from the chrysanthemums still clinging to his nose. He lay down on the rug and I turned my full attention to the interview.

'And is Emma still healthy, Sheila? How old is she now?'

I was just about to tell Shelley that she was well and happy, when the audience began to laugh. What had I done? I hadn't made a joke. I looked round to see two dear old ladies on the front row almost doubled up with laughter. It was bound to be Bracken. It was Bracken. He had a mouth full of sheepskin rug and he was trying to drag it off with him. I was pretty sure he wouldn't succeed because Shelley and I were sitting on it but the noises he was making, the barks and muffled growls of threats to kill, were enough to make anybody laugh.

'Er . . . where was I? Yes,' I said to Shelley. I knew the answer must be yes or no but I couldn't remember what it was. By this time Shelley was laughing as well.

'Bracken, leave it,' I whispered. I tried to prise him off the rug but the more I pulled, the more vehement he became that he was going to get the better of this thing, whatever it was. There was only a very short time for the interview and needless to say it came to an end before I had a chance to say much at all, but the audience enjoyed it. I hope the people at home could see what was happening. Luckily for me, the end of my interview marked a commercial break so I was able to drag Bracken off the rug – no easy feat I can tell you – which was a little soggy and minus a few tufts of wool. Bracken walked reluctantly off the set, ears drooping, a sulky expression on his face and dragging his back feet along behind him. Don was still laughing when we walked out of the studio.

'Well, petal, I don't think you did your book any good. You didn't say much about it at all, did you? But the audience enjoyed it and Bracken certainly did. We'd better hurry up, we're meeting Harold and Betty soon. I don't think there's much more mischief Bracken can get up to today.'

He was wrong . . .

Harold and Betty were waiting for us at the car park in Hull. They are always early. So prompt. I wish I could manage to do that. I seem to live in a chaos of being late.

'It's not far from here,' Harold said, after the usual greetings. 'You can take the car round if you like, Don.'

'Oh no, let's walk,' I said. 'It'll be much nicer and it will give Bracken a bit of exercise.'

Betty immediately fell in behind with Don and Harold took my arm. He knew I could see but he always felt the need to look after me. 'There's a kerb here, Sheila. One step down, just a little one.'

I looked at him and smiled. 'Yes, Harold.' We walked across the road.

'Oh, mind that post. Come this way.'

'It's all right, Harold. Honestly.'

'Oh, I keep forgetting,' he said. 'I always want to look after you.'

'I don't mind, Harold. It's very kind of you.'

But he just couldn't help himself. He just went on telling me when we reached the kerbs, whether they were up or down, taking me round posts, stopping when people were in the way and however much I insisted I could see, he wouldn't have it. He just chuckled at me and said he liked doing it. It reminded me of the time we went on holiday with Harold and Betty. We were in Cornwall – before I could see, that is – and Harold and Don decided that they'd like lobster for dinner. I'd never had it before.

'You'll love it,' Harold kept telling me. 'You really will. It's the best fish you can have and I've told them we want a really good one.'

I was looking forward to it, but when it arrived that evening I took one mouthful and decided I didn't like lobster after all. But I couldn't tell Harold – he'd already made sure that all the fish was cut up and everything was right for me

33

on my plate. I can't say that I liked people to cut things up for me when I was blind. I appreciated it if they told me where things were on my plate. Using the plate as a clock made it quite easy: peas at twelve, chips at three and fish at nine. But Harold enjoyed cutting everything up for me so I let him do it.

'Do you like it?' Don asked.

'Y-yes. It's . . . very nice.' Don knew from the way I said it that I wasn't awfully keen. Harold, on the other hand, was absolutely delighted.

'Do you like it, Sheila? I knew you would. I'm so glad I ordered it for you. Perhaps we could have another before we go.'

'Oh! Y-yes, Harold. It's – er – very nice.'

Betty was silently munching away. I think she'd caught the intonation in my voice. I went on eating lobster. On and on. It never seemed to come to an end, lobster every mouthful. I must have had three giant lobsters on my plate. It almost made me feel ill. I only ate it to please Harold and had to remember, at every mouthful, to say how really delicious it was and how pleased I was that he'd ordered it for me. It wasn't until a few hours later, when Don and I were alone, that he told me.

'You didn't like the lobster, did you, Sheila?'

'No, not really, but I couldn't disappoint Harold, could I?'

'I know, but I felt very sorry because he kept giving you pieces of his lobster. He thought you were enjoying it so much, he hardly had any himself. He gave you nearly all his and he pinched a bit off Betty's plate for you as well.'

'Oh no!' I said. 'Why didn't you stop him?'

'Well, petal, I couldn't. It gave him so much pleasure to see you eating it.'

That was Harold.

'Here's the book shop, Sheila.' Harold held my arm a little tighter. 'Mind the step, it's a big one. Now then, where do we go? Ah, here's your display of books and a seat. There you are, you sit down. I'll take your coat.' He took my coat off and went to find somewhere to hang it.

'I think Don and I will go and have a look round the shops, Sheila,' Betty said. 'You'll be all right?'

'Yes, I'll be fine, Betty.' Knowing that Harold would stay.

Don and Betty went off to do the shopping, and Harold was soon back with the manager of the shop.

'Here we are, Sheila. I've found the manager for you.'

Introductions over, the signing session began. Harold stood at the back of the chair, occasionally patting me on the shoulder and asking me if all was well.

'Do you want a cup of tea?' he asked me.

'Not at the moment, Harold.'

'Well, if there's anything you want, just ask me. I'm here at the back of you.'

'Thank you, Harold.'

'Is the old lad okay?' he asked, looking down at Bracken who was curled up under the table fast asleep.

'Yes, he's fine.'

'Do you think he'd like a bowl of water or should I take him for a walk?'

'No, don't worry, Harold. He'll be quite happy under there.'

Bracken appeared to be sleeping but now I realize he was waiting. Most of the people who came up to have their books signed popped their shopping bags down on the floor and this was what Bracken was waiting for. While I was signing books, he was rummaging into everybody's shopping basket to see if there was anything interesting there. And he found something very interesting in one lady's shopping bag: a loaf of bread. One of those big long French loaves. I was so busy signing books, I didn't realize until Harold tapped my shoulder.

'Sheila,' he whispered, 'the old lad, he's got a loaf under the table and he's eating it.

'What!' I said, dropping my pen and book on the table. 'Good grief! Bracken, leave it alone!' I managed to salvage half the loaf from him, picked it up and put it on the table. 'Is this anyone's bread?' I called.

One poor lady waiting in the queue looked horrified. 'It was my French loaf,' she said.

35

'Oh gosh, I'm awfully sorry, the dog's eaten it.'

'Don't worry,' she said. 'It'll do. I didn't want the whole of it anyway.'

I was amazed as she took it off the table, wrapped it up in some paper and put it back in her bag. 'It'll do me for tea,' she said, and off she went.

That's Yorkshire people through and through. Practical to the last, unperturbed by anything and always friendly. After the signing session Betty insisted we go back for a meal. A Yorkshire meal is what we midlanders and southerners would probably refer to as a banquet and, sure enough, it was. Everything had been prepared. In the corner the table was groaning with the weight of the food: flans, trifles, cakes, sausage rolls, fresh ham, pickles, lettuce, tomatoes . . . it was a beautiful spread. Betty set to making me a cup of tea while Harold put the plates out. We'd no sooner started eating when a knock came at the door. It turned out to be a delivery man.

'Come in,' Betty said. 'Come in and have a cup of tea.'

He was introduced all round as Bill and he had hardly sat down before Betty put a cup of tea in his hand. Harold grabbed a plate and sized up the table. 'Now, old lad, what are you going to have to eat?'

'Eee, I've just had me dinner, Harold.'

'Never mind your dinner, look at this lot,' Harold said.

It was always a challenge to him to make people eat as much as they possibly could, and he and Betty would have been mortally offended if anyone had gone in and gone out of their house without having a good meal. Sausage rolls and ham were piled on to Bill's plate. Cakes and trifle followed. The poor man could hardly move, let alone continue his round, by the time Harold and Betty had plied him with food and tea.

It was when the alcohol started to flow that I became worried. Harold took a bottle out of the little cupboard in the kitchen that was stocked full of whisky, home-made wine, beer – anything you care to mention – and looked eagerly at Don, grinning.

'Now then, old lad' (Harold calls anything male 'old lad').
'What are you gonna have to drink?'

'Oh no, Harold, I mustn't. Got to drive back.'

I knew it was fatal. I tried to get up and make a dash for
the car but I didn't make it in time. Put Harold, Don and
alcohol together and it has a similar effect to throwing a
gallon of petrol on a dying fire. I remember one Christmas –
well, Betty and I remember one Christmas and we're the
only two who do – we spent up there. For days after we'd
arrived home, Don would ask me things like, 'Who bought
me that tie, petal?'; 'Where did this bottle of whisky come
from?'; 'What did we do on Christmas Eve?'

CHAPTER FOUR

'I'M SURE SHE'S going to have them tonight,' I said to Don.

'No, she won't. Now go back to sleep.'

'I can't.' I sat on the edge of the bed. I was waiting for Buttons to have her first litter of puppies.

'They're not due yet,' Don told me.

'I know, but it's no good. I can't rest. I'll go down and sit with her.' I sat with her that night and the night after, but nothing happened.

The puppies had been due on Emma's birthday, the 16th October, and, as luck would have it, a friend of mine, Caroline Whitlock, was staying with us. Caroline breeds chocolate Labradors and knows all about delivering puppies. When she arrived at tea-time on the Wednesday I was in a state of nervous exhaustion.

'Oh, Caroline, I'm so pleased you've arrived.'

'Why?' she said. 'Has she had her litter yet?'

'No, that's just the point. Come and have a look at her. Tell me what you think.'

Buttons was sitting in what is called our Dog Room, which is a type of utility room off the kitchen.

'Yes, I think she's going to have them tonight,' Caroline told me.

'Mm, I've already spent two nights sitting waiting.'

'You are a silly.' She smiled at me. 'I told you she wouldn't have them till I arrived, didn't I? Now what we'll do is take it in turns. If she hasn't had any puppies by bedtime, we'll split the night up into shifts.'

'That's a good idea. At least I can get some sleep.'

Buttons produced her first little chocolate puppy at half-past ten. It was quite simple: she just had the puppy. She looked at it a bit strangely at first, with a quizzical look on her face as if to say, Where did that come from? But she soon settled down to nursing it. She'd had two puppies by the time Caroline went to bed. I stayed up until one o'clock when the third puppy arrived, a little yellow one. Two chocolates and one yellow. When I dragged myself out of bed at six o'clock in the morning, I was just in time to see the last puppy of six arrive – another yellow. So we had four chocolate and two yellow puppies. No matter how many litters I witness being born, the miracle of new life never ceases to amaze me. They were beautiful. Little Emmas.

I spent Thursday morning ringing everyone to tell them of our happy arrivals. Most people were queuing up to come and have a look at them, especially those who had ordered puppies. Deirdre was the first one on the scene that evening, bringing her two children, Sean and Katherine. Deirdre was to have a chocolate male puppy from the litter, unbeknown to John, her husband. That first night she and the children stood watching the puppies snuggle up to Buttons and listening to their little squeaking noises.

'I can't wait to take mine home,' Deirdre said. 'Won't it be lovely to have a puppy about the house?'

They'd never had a dog, but the children had always wanted one. They were almost grown up now, teenagers in fact.

'What about John?' I asked. 'Have you told him yet?'

'No. I'm not going to say anything to him. Every time I mention us having a dog, he says no, they're too much of a responsibility and he might let me have one sometime in the future.'

'Oh dear, I don't know whether I'd risk that.'

'It's the only way,' Deirdre told me. 'Just to appear one night with one. He won't make me bring him back, I know he won't. He'll love him just as much as we will.'

Over the next few weeks I had to be very careful when John came round that I didn't mention anything about the puppy Deirdre had ordered. The puppies grew not so much into little Emmas as into little bundles of terror and mischief.

They almost ate me out of house and home and there wasn't much housework done in that time. I spent most of it sitting with the puppies getting to know their characters, watching them turn into expressive creatures. I became so attached to each and every one of them that it was heart-breaking when they had to go. But I was very fortunate in the fact that all the litter had been spoken for by people I knew, barring one and she was going to be a guide-dog. I was really thrilled about that. The Guide-Dogs for the Blind Association breed a lot of their own puppies. Their brood bitches are kept as pets by various people who live around the Training Centres, and they usually go there to have their litters. Sometimes they need extra puppies and it was at this time they were looking around, so I was able to let them have one of Buttons' puppies. They don't just take any Labrador puppy, of course. Derek Freeman, who looks after all the breeding and puppy walking side of the Guide-Dogs, chooses his stock very carefully. He wanted to see the pedigrees of both mum and dad – Bracken being the father – to examine them not only for type and temperament, but to see if there were any hidden diseases, such as what we call PRA (progressive retinal atrophy), a disease which attacks the retina of the eye. As the dog grows older, it gradually goes blind – not the sort of thing you can afford to have in a working guide-dog. But both Buttons and Bracken came from impeccable stock and so their puppy was accepted.

I was very excited the day that I was taking the puppy to the Training Centre. I hadn't been to the Leamington Spa Guide-Dog Training Centre since I came home with Emma so I knew, for me, it would be a very emotional experience. Betty, my friend from round the corner, had offered to drive me down, not only because she's very good in that way but also because she was interested in seeing the Guide-Dog Training Centre too.

It was a beautiful sunny day when we took the puppy down, and the autumn leaves were still on the ground. It had been sunny the first time when I went for Emma in

July 1966. I looked with keen interest as we drove through Leamington itself.

'What's that road called?' I asked Betty. (I don't have distance or detailed vision so I couldn't see the street names.)

'That's The Parade,' she said.

'Emma and I used to walk along there. Across the lights, across the crossing and then into a park. Can you see a park up there?'

'Yes, it has flower gardens in it.'

'That's the one. Well, you go straight past The Parade,' I told her, 'straight down Warwick New Road and you'll see the Centre.'

It brought back so many memories. I could even remember how many down kerbs it was from the Training Centre into The Parade in Leamington Spa. That's the sort of thing you have to remember as a blind person . . . how many roads you've crossed and where to turn left or right. But it was many years since I last said 'Forward' to Emma. The Training Centre itself was a beautiful place. Up the drive and on to the Tudor style house, into the reception hall where I stood all those years ago, shaking in nervous anticipation. This time Betty and I stood there, the little puppy clutched in my arms. She was my offering to them. My exchange for Emma. She was six weeks old, and was to be collected from the Training Centre by her puppy walker. She would spend a year learning the basic training before going back to the Centre to be taught to be a guide-dog. It would be quite a time before I knew whether she had actually passed her final test or not. I just hoped she'd make someone as a good a guide-dog as Emma had made me.

Derek was there to meet us and, as he knew that it was my first sighted visit to the Training Centre, he offered to show me round. First of all the kennels, full of lovely Labradors living in comfort. I've never seen such beautiful kennels and I'm sure I never will. Then the house itself, where I saw the lounge that Emma and I used to sit in night after night. It was all so different from how I'd imagined it as a blind person, and odd to actually see where the doors were and where the radio sat on the shelf, but now they had put a clock on the mantelpiece. 'You didn't have that there,' I said, 'not in 1966.'

'No,' Derek laughed. 'We didn't. We put it there for the ticking.'

'What do you mean?' I said.

'Well, it's a good piece to listen to, so that you can orientate yourself in the room.'

'Oh, yes, that's a good idea.' I realized I'd stopped thinking as a blind person. I didn't have to use my ears any more when I went into a room. 'Can I go and have a look at the bedrooms?' I asked.

'Yes, of course. You know where they are, don't you?'

Yes, I remembered. Through the lounge door, turn left, find the mat at the bottom of the stairs – and up I went. It was so much easier with sight. I didn't have to feel for the mat. I found my bedroom. There it was with its old braille number on. Luckily it was unoccupied so I could go in and sit on the bed. I imagined someone else sitting there, being introduced to the little chocolate puppy I'd brought, and I hoped it would give them freedom. I don't mind admitting that, as Betty and I drove away and I looked back on the house, it was a very misty picture I saw through my tears. It had brought back so many memories, both of pain and happiness, but most of all of Emma. Emma as a young dog. A sprightly little Labrador who would bounce up and down at my door waiting for me to put the harness on so she could take me out. She was always so keen to get wherever we were going, she was always wanting to learn new places and new tricks. I remembered how both Emma and I would look forward to our dinner-time walks in the forest near where I worked: once I'd let Emma off the harness I'd hear her paws scudding on the grass as she ran backwards and forwards to fetch me sticks and things to throw for her, coming back every moment or so to touch me with her nose to tell me that she was still there. Then I thought of Bracken and Buttons and their young days. They'd never be guide-dogs but at least one of their puppies had gone to be one and that made me feel very good inside.

42

CHAPTER FIVE

ONE THURSDAY EVENING Deirdre arrived to collect her puppy. She was carrying a little basket to put him in. At six weeks old, he was very small. I'd nicknamed him Gingerfoot because he had some mismarking on his paws. Instead of being all chocolate, he had ginger bits.

'Have you told John?' I asked as soon as she walked through the door.

'No, I haven't. He's not in this evening. He won't be back until about half-past-eleven. Don't worry, he'll be all right.'

'I *am* worried though. I really don't feel you've done the right thing.'

'You know he wouldn't let me have a puppy,' she told me. 'I've been asking him for years and I just feel that I've reached the stage now where I really need one. You know Katherine's going away, don't you?'

'Yes, she's starting university soon, isn't she?'

'The house will be so lonely without her. I feel the need for something small and cuddly to love. I want something to be at home that needs me.'

I well understood her feelings. I packed a diet sheet, Gingerfoot's pedigree and some food for him, and she put him into the basket. She was smiling all over her face as she walked down the drive.

'Bye, Sheila. Don't worry, it'll be all right.'

But I couldn't help worrying. I sat in front of the television that night but didn't see anything that was on. I couldn't stop thinking about what would happen when John arrived home. When the last programme finished I was still sitting there. I looked across at Don. 'John'll be home by now, won't he? The phone hasn't rung. Nobody's come to the front door.' It was a quarter to twelve. 'Do you think we should sit up a little longer in case he brings the puppy back?'

'No, he won't bring the puppy back. You know what John is, he really loves dogs.'

I knew John did. He was always coming to see the puppies and making a fuss of my dogs and cats. He was really an old softy, and I couldn't understand why he'd been so firm about not letting Deirdre have a puppy. But I still went to bed that night with a feeling of foreboding. When nine o'clock came the next morning, I was beginning to relax. Then the front doorbell rang. I opened the door to see Deirdre standing there, the puppy in the basket, tears streaming down her face.

'Oh, Deirdre, what's happened, what's the matter?'

'John!' she said. 'He won't let me have him. He's made me bring him back. He told me that I must ask him first.'

I felt so upset, not only for Deirdre but for the puppy, who'd had one night in another home and then had to be brought back to his mum. When I put him down next to Buttons, he looked startled and surprised. He didn't quite know what to do.

'Couldn't you persuade him?' I said to Deirdre. 'It seems so terrible.'

'No, I can't. If he says I can't have one, I can't and that's it,' she sobbed. 'It's no good, I must respect his wishes.'

She spoke very highly of John, even at that moment. I felt very bitter towards him. I wanted to ring him up and tell him what I really thought of him. How could he do this to his wife, his lovely wife who thought the world of him and would do anything he asked? And so respected him that she'd even bring the puppy back, the puppy that she'd picked from the day he was born and had so loved over the six weeks she'd been to see him? There were no smiles this time as Deirdre left the house and went down the drive. She could hardly say a word. I heard her slam the car door and the engine start. When Don came in for his lunch, it upset me to tell him what had happened. He could hardly believe it.

'It would be different if he didn't like dogs,' I said to Don, 'but he does. I can't understand him.'

Don, Sheila and Kerensa with Bracken and Ming.

(from left) Shadow, Teak, Buttons, Bracken - and Mocha with her back to the camera. Trust Mocha.

Bracken answering the telephone.

'Well, you know what John is,' Don told me. 'He likes to be the man of his house.'

'He is!' I said. 'He must realize that or Deirdre wouldn't have brought the puppy back, would she? She would have ignored him.'

I spent the whole of Friday really hating John and vowing that I'd never speak to him again, nor let him come and see our puppies in the future. I couldn't understand how anyone could be so cruel. You can imagine how I felt when, early on Saturday morning, the doorbell rang and I opened the door to see John. Luckily for me, I was speechless at seeing him there or I might have said something I would have later regretted. Then I noticed the basket in his hand that Deirdre had fetched and brought the puppy back in. I was astonished. 'Yes?' I said to him coldly. 'What do you want?'

'I've come for the puppy,' he told me cheerfully. Sean followed him in.

'What do you mean, you've come for the puppy?'

'I've relented. She can have the puppy. Where is he? I'll take him straight back.' John was all smiles and cheerfulness as he fetched the puppy from Buttons. Sean, in the meantime, took me in the lounge and whispered, 'Mum's been so upset about it. She couldn't eat anything yesterday. I think she spent all night up pining for him. She so loves him you know.'

'Yes, I know,' I told him. 'Why has your Dad changed his mind?'

'I think he realized how much Mum wanted that puppy. He didn't understand before, and it's not that he doesn't like dogs, you know. He does. He wanted to be the one to make the decision to have a puppy, that's all.'

'He will love him,' I asked Sean, 'won't he? He will look after him? He won't resent him, will he?'

'Goodness me, no,' Sean said. 'You mark my words, Dad'll be as daft as a brush with that dog.'

Sure enough, as John came back into the lounge with the puppy cuddled in his arms, he was whispering into his ear, telling him what a lovely home he was going to.

45

Most of Buttons' litter had been given away to friends. That was reassuring because I knew they were all going to be looked after and loved. Betty, my friend round the corner, had one. John and Deirdre, of course. And one had gone in the hopes of being a guide-dog. The other three were found homes locally so I could keep an eye on them. They were all like children to me. I don't mean that I'm sentimental about dogs, but I do care what happens if I sell a puppy. There are so many uncared for dogs, so many dogs left to roam the streets. It's not difficult when people come to buy puppies to assess whether they'll look after their dog or not. Of course, we can always be wrong, but in most cases I can tell whether a prospective owner will really care for their dog or not. I give as much help and advice as I possibly can and always tell my owners to take their dogs to a Dog Training Club. From lack of knowledge, people aren't able to train their dogs. A trained dog – and its owner of course – is so much happier. I don't think I've ever yet seen a miserable working dog, and my own experiences with Emma tell me that a dog loves to work. Emma really enjoyed having her harness on and looked forward to taking me out every morning. Of course, she was a guide-dog and she needed me as much as I needed her. She taught me an awful lot about dog-behaviour. If I respected her wishes, she respected mine. If a dog is treated with respect and intelligence then you can't go far wrong.

In all the years that Emma and I worked together, I only remember one occasion when she didn't want to take me out. It was a January evening and on reaching home from work we were both wet through and very cold. It was sleeting and a gale was blowing outside. As soon as Emma had eaten her dinner – that was always the first thing I did when I came in from work, my tea had to wait – she settled herself in front of the gas fire, curled up and went to sleep. I had a talk to give. I went out quite a lot in those days to various organizations, such as WIs and Townswomen's Guilds, to give talks about guide-dogs. I felt it was my way, not only of helping the Association to raise money, but also of showing how independent and worthwhile a blind person's life could be. I was always fighting the battle for equality. Because I was blind, most people thought I was unable to do a job of work, and probably that I was deaf as well because I was always shouted at when I arrived at my venue. It was a very important part of my life with Emma, and this particular evening I had a talk out of Nottingham which meant my catching a bus into town from where I lived, going into the bus station and taking another bus out again. I had a quick bite to eat, put my coat back on and began feeling for Emma's harness – always the signal for Emma to come rushing to the front door and bounce around in excitement. But this time there was no response! 'Emma,' I called. She still didn't come. I became quite worried. I went back into the lounge and felt in front of the gas fire. There she was, fast asleep, snoring her head off. I gave her a little tap.

'Emma, we must go out. We have a talk.'

Emma loved going on talks. She'd race to the bus stop and be first on the bus. She knew that once we arrived she'd get lots of people to admire her and say how brilliant she was. This time she never stirred. I began to think she was ill. I felt her nose: that was nice and cold. Her paws and her ears were warm. (That's always a sign of good health with a dog.)

'Emma, come on,' I said, 'quickly. We must catch that bus.'

She put her head up and nuzzled me with her nose. 'I don't want to come,' was what she was telling me, and put her head down again.

'I'm sorry, Emma. I know it's awful out there but we really have to go.'

I always talked to Emma the same as I would a person. I think this is one of the reasons why we had such a close relationship. I treated her as a human being and I really do believe she thought she was one. Eventually I managed to persuade her that we were going out. I put her harness and collar and lead on and walked down the path. The sleet was biting into my face. I had my hood well wrapped round my ears and my eyes closed against the stinging rain and snow.

If there's one thing that puts a blind person off direction, it's a howling gale. I really had to listen to where I was going, apart from remembering how many kerbs to cross and where to give Emma the instructions for going right or left. It's a partnership when you work with a guide-dog. I can only equate it to driving a car – neither one is any good without the other. It was easy to get to the bus stop. I only had to cross one intersection and turn left at the next, then it was about twenty paces up the road. I didn't seem to have crossed an intersection and I felt sure that I should have got to it by now.

'Emma, find the bus stop,' I repeated, just as a reminder. But she didn't. After about ten minutes of walking, she stopped and sat down. I put my hand out to feel the bus stop but it wasn't there. I was back at my own garden gate. Emma had taken me the full circle round the block, back home again.

'That won't do,' I told her. 'Look, I know you don't want to go out and I know it's terribly cold but all those ladies are sitting there waiting for us to appear and we can't let them down.'

As if appealing to her better nature had made her think again, she got up and went back up the road. We had crossed the intersection this time and when we got to the next left turn, Emma sat down. I felt sure we hadn't gone far enough. It was usually about twenty paces once we'd turned left. It's amazing how much you remember as a blind person: how many paces to here, how many intersections you've crossed, where the bus stops, where shops are – by smell or by sound. I put my hand up again. No, I wasn't at the bus stop. I was at the letter-box this time, and I knew that was only a few yards away from the bus stop. Emma was trying every trick in the book to fool me.

'No, Emma. Find the bus stop.'

Eventually we made it to the post. My stop was the one before the terminus in town, which would leave me near the bus station. Emma knew the way, of course. Across the main road, under a subway and come out in the bus station and all

I had to say to her was Mount Street bus station. She knew all the three separate bus stations in Nottingham just by name. Once off the bus at the allotted place, I told Emma to find the kerb and then the subway. Again, I thought it was rather strange. We had to cross a major road and then make a right turn into the subway. I'd certainly crossed a road but, to me, it had only seemed a small one. But who was I to argue with Emma? I couldn't see where I was going and there was still that terrible howling gale to contend with and, as I said, it does put a blind person off. I had completely lost my sense of direction. But Emma marched on. I could feel her tail wagging. Oh good, I thought, she's pleased we're going on a talk now she's out. She sat down with great fervour and gave a snort. 'Good girl, Emma. Are we in the bus station?'

'Hello, me duck, are you all right?' It turned out to be a bus driver – the bus driver that had brought us into Nottingham and dropped us off a few minutes earlier. He'd then turned the bus round into the depot to wait to go back to where I lived at Beechdale.

'Where am I?' I asked him.

'Well, me duck, you've just got off round the corner. What are you doing round here? I'm going back to Beechdale. Have you changed your mind?'

'No, I haven't,' I said. 'I'm supposed to be at Mount Street bus station. Emma's changed her mind, she wants to go home again.'

He gave a hearty laugh. 'That dog knows better than we do. It's not fit for a dog on a night like this, is it, me duck? Do you want any help getting to the bus station?'

'No,' I said. 'I think she'll admit defeat now. Emma, come on, find Mount Street bus station.'

Emma eventually gave in and we did get to our talk on time. We were both very wet and cold but we had a lovely warm reception from the ladies and I think they made up to Emma for her coming out on that really horrible night.

CHAPTER SIX

'I COULD REALLY settle there. Could you?' Don was looking over a large 'For Sale' board that jutted out of the hedge to Rose Cottage.

'Of course,' I told him. I could settle anywhere. If there were boarding kennels going for sale in the middle of the Sahara Desert I'd go. We both desperately wanted to move out into the country, away from suburbia. To me suburbia had become a 'no man's land' where people just slept. The houses in the daytime were deserted while everyone was away at the city earning their living, busy with shops and factories. The country too would be busy, but with animals and birds, the sound of corn rustling in open fields. That was where I wanted to live. Because of increasing rules and regulations suburbia had become a place of emptiness, at least to me. We'd been turned down to run our boarding cattery in our suburban garden because businesses weren't the thing where we lived, not that sort of business anyway. There was a time – even I remember – when people kept chickens in their back garden, but nowadays you're only allowed to prune your roses. I felt a deep sadness for those people who had to lock their doors in the morning and catch the buses to the city. At least I could be free. Free to choose when I wanted to do my work. It meant I could enjoy the beautiful days and the scenery around me and get out to take in every inch of the countryside, perhaps because I appreciate it more than other people. I had time to stand in the fields and watch the rabbits play and listen to the birds sing. I'm one of the lucky ones.

I stared at the cottage nestled in the green fields. Yes, I could easily settle here with my dogs around me. We both wanted to run boarding kennels. I was very lucky to have met Don, not only because he's such a nice person, but because his ideas always coincide with mine. I've always loved dogs and had a longing to run boarding kennels. I don't know why, because it's all hard work and worry but I have a need to look after dogs and I, for one, can't bear the thought of going on holiday and leaving my dogs in kennels. So I feel that it's up to me to run the sort of kennels and cattery that people wouldn't mind leaving their pets in. Don, who I'm sure had no intention of ever running any boarding kennels, had come round to my way of thinking. Because of his great love for our dogs he'd become more and more interested in them. And he, too, was beginning to feel the suffocation of house-upon-house, garden-upon-garden.

Don edged the car slowly up the drive to Rose Cottage. 'Look that's the paddock on the right!' he said. 'We could build the kennels there, then we could make a car park at the top, tarmac all this drive . . . it would be a lot easier. What do you think about setting poplars along that line, wouldn't that look lovely?'

Don had got it all set out in his mind. We hadn't even looked round the house yet. 'Oh, it would,' I agreed with him. 'It would look perfect.'

Don pulled the car round the house, stopped, leaned over the steering wheel and gazed into the distance. 'Look at that view. Isn't it fantastic?'

I was getting out of the car, eager to look round the house.

'Come in, come in,' Mrs Adams welcomed us. 'I'm sorry it isn't a very nice day. It looks much more beautiful in the sunshine.'

We always seemed to look at houses when it was dull or raining, but that didn't put us off this one and when I saw the kitchen . . . it was a positive housewife's dream – fitted units, double sinks and large picture windows where I could visualize myself looking over the fields while I washed up. I could see cows standing across the other side of the garden fence mooing gently. Their sound gave me a feeling of tranquillity and timelessness. It wouldn't seem half as much of a chore as it did at the moment, staring out to another brick wall. There was only one thing wrong with the house as far as Don and I could see, and that was the indoor swimming pool. We didn't want a swimming pool. It seemed a waste to us of time, money and space. I'd got ideas of turning that into an indoor cattery.

'Yes, we like it very much,' Don told Mrs Adams. 'All we need now is the planning permission to have our boarding kennels here.'

'Oh, I'm sure you won't have any trouble getting that. After all, it's right out in the country. You can't be bothering anyone, can you, with dogs here?'

I wasn't so sure, having been up against our local council once before. Again, the planning forms poured in – they're almost as bad as tax forms. We filled them in and sent them back and dreamed. Dreamed of what it would be like out in the country and of how we'd build the kennels. Don spent most evenings drawing plans up.

'What do you think of this one?' he said. 'If we had some standard rose trees along that row of kennels there it'd look lovely. In fact, we could put some seats out. You could sit there in the summer.'

I laughed. 'I won't have time to sit there in the summer if all those kennels are full, will I?'

'Mm, no. Well I could sit there,' he said jokingly.

I knew he wouldn't have time. We're both the same, Don and I. We think the same and we do the same and we love working. I could imagine nothing more heavenly than us both working together. But our dreams were shattered when, a few weeks later, we had the reply from the Planning Office. No, they wouldn't give us permission for boarding kennels there, owing to various objections they had received from people living around the area. One of the objectors had put forward the idea that dogs could escape and run riot round the country.

'I want to run boarding kennels,' I said to Don, 'not a compound for killer dogs!'

'And then there was the traffic problem . . .' the council's letter went on. 'Residents are objecting to the noise that the many cars coming up and down the road would bring.'

That made me smile. 'Anybody would think they'd be coming in bus loads and droves, boarding their dogs with us.' If only we had a right of reply to these things, I could have explained that probably most of our clients' pets would have been collected and delivered. There would have been hardly any traffic at all, and what there would have been we were going to cater for by our own car park.

'Oh well,' I said to Don, throwing the letter in the waste bin, 'back to the evening papers.' I found consolation in the fact that at least I could take the dogs out and get my daily dose of the countryside before returning to suburbia. Buttons and Bracken would race around like motorbikes, while Emma – when I took her with me – would sedately sniff each blade of grass. There was a time, not so long ago, when Emma could easily walk four miles over the fields and still did not look as tired as Buttons or Bracken, but these days she often didn't come with me. She decided that the best place was at home asleep on the carpet. Of course she was slowing down. I'd begun to notice it but I wouldn't accept the fact. I pretended she just didn't feel like it today, would rather stop in and she'd probably want to come tomorrow. Emma slowed down to such an extent that I began to get quite worried about her. Yes, she was sixteen, a very old lady. Most dogs didn't make it to that age, but Emma was different. Emma would go on forever, I told myself. But I had that nagging fear at the back of my mind that I could never voice to anyone: Emma was slowing down too much and too fast. She wasn't taking an interest in what was going on around her. She didn't get up to make a fuss of anyone that came in. Even her food was losing its appeal.

The crunch came one Saturday night. Don and I had been watching a thriller film on television and it was about one o'clock when I switched the set off and prepared to put the dogs out into the garden for their last walk round. I went to open the back door. 'Everyone out!' I called. They knew that command. It was a nightly ritual and they'd all rush to the back door to have their last smell of the night air before settling down. Buttons and Bracken ran out into the garden but there was no sign of Emma. I closed the back door and went into the lounge. She was still fast asleep near the chair where I'd been sitting. 'Come on, Emma. It's everybody out time.' I gave her a stroke. She never made a noise or attempted to get up. 'There's a good girl, come on.' I knelt down on the carpet. 'What's the matter?'

After a while she tried to raise herself off the floor, but she couldn't seem to get on to her back legs. I helped her up and she staggered about the lounge as if she was in a daze, not knowing quite where she was or what she wanted. I guided her slowly into the kitchen but the floor was too much for her. It was slippery and she kept falling over. Inwardly I wanted to run away from the situation, to run screaming from the house, to pretend that it wasn't happening and leave Don to deal with it, but I knew that it was me that had to be there to help her. She didn't want to go out. Instead, she went to the water bowl. She stood over it as if gazing into its depths, trying to drink from it but unable to. I looked at my watch. It was one-thirty in the morning but it didn't matter. I had to ring the vet. Don was standing at the kitchen door.

'Oh, poor girl. What's the matter with her?'

'I don't know. Will you come over here and watch her. I'll go and ring the vet.'

'Her tummy looks strange,' Don commented as he went towards her. 'Have you noticed? Look, it's like a balloon.'

I took one glance and then dashed for the phone. 'Come on, hurry up and answer,' I urged, almost before I'd finished dialling the number. It rang and rang. 'You've got to be there,' I said. 'You're a vet, you've got to be there.' At last a sleepy voice said hello. It sounded like a young girl to me. 'Are you the vet?' I almost screamed.

'Yes, what is it?'

'You must come out. It's Emma. There's something terribly wrong with her, you must come out.'

'Yes, all right, I will. What's the address?'

54

I gabbled it to her. 'I'll look out for you,' I said. 'I'll stand at the bottom of the drive.'

'Don't worry. I know where you live,' she said and put down the phone.

'Are they coming?' Don called from the kitchen.

'Yes. I think I got her out of bed.'

'Which vet was it?'

I went to a practice where there were about six vets. 'Don't know. Didn't recognize her voice.'

'I hope she's good,' Don muttered.

So did I.

CHAPTER SEVEN

IT SEEMED AN eternity as I stared out of the lounge window into the empty darkness, watching for headlights, listening for the sound of a car. Don had helped Emma back into the lounge, where she'd flopped back down on to the carpet.

'Why doesn't she come?' I groaned.

'Shall I put the kettle on?' Don asked, always practical. 'I'm sure she'll want a drink and I bet you could do with a cup of tea, couldn't you?'

'Yes, yes I could. Let me do it,' I said. I had to keep my mind occupied. I filled the kettle slowly, meticulously put it in the right place and plugged it in, emptied the teapot and then decided to give it a wash for good measure.

'She's here!' Don shouted from the front door.

I flung the teapot on to the draining board and rushed down the hall. 'Thank God', I said to myself. It's at times like these when you begin to think of your vet as almost a God. They are the people who really matter in the world – I expect them to work miracles, to conjure up magic from their little black bag. But, as I greeted my vet on the doorstep, my heart began to sink. She seemed a young girl to me, probably only twenty-three or twenty-four, long brown hair, very slightly built. She didn't look as if she could lift a poodle on to an examination table, let alone treat a Labrador. But, nevertheless, I urged her to come in the hall.

'It's Emma,' I said. 'She's in the lounge. There's something terribly wrong with her.'

'Let's have a look, shall we?' She was still dishevelled from sleep. Obviously I'd dragged her out of bed. 'What's the matter with her, what are the symptoms?'

'She couldn't get up on to her back legs and when she managed to she fell over again. She made for the water bowl but didn't drink anything, she just stared blindly into it. And look at her tummy – it's huge. Can you do something, what's the matter with her?' I was sure this young slip of a girl wouldn't be able to diagnose a cold. Why hadn't they sent someone else, someone older, one of the other vets who had treated Emma before?

'There's a good girl, Emma,' she said in a calm, sleepy voice. She fondled her ears and stroked her head before examining her tummy. She reached for a stethoscope out of her bag. 'Mm, her heart's strong enough. That's one good thing.' After taking Emma's temperature and looking into her mouth, she sat back on the carpet. 'Well, it looks as if there's a lot of gas in there. She's either eaten something that's really upset her or there's a virus that's attacking her.'

'Can you do anything?' I pleaded. 'Will she be all right?'

'I'll give her an injection and see if that does the trick.' She pulled out a syringe and a bottle from her black bag and injected Emma. 'I'll wait a little while to see what happens.' She closed her bag up and sat on the settee.

'Would you like a cup of tea?' Don asked. 'I've just made one.'

'Yes, please.'

'I'm sorry, we don't know your name,' Don said.

'Gwen.'

'Well, Gwen, do you take sugar?'

'No, thank you. Nice and strong, it might wake me up a bit.'

I was still a little unsure of Gwen's qualifications and wondered if she was good enough to treat Emma, but I tried to relax. 'I'm sorry for getting you out of bed,' I said, 'but it was urgent.'

'Oh yes, don't worry about that. One of the hazards of our profession.'

'Have you just qualified?' I asked. 'I haven't seen you before.'

'Yes, I've not been here long. My first job, actually.'

My heart began to sink again. 'Have you treated many Labradors?'

'Quite a few. How old is Emma now?'

'She's over sixteen,' I told her. 'An old lady really but I'm sure she has plenty of life in her yet.' I said it to reassure myself more than anyone else. Gwen sipped her tea and looked anxiously across at Emma. Don tried to keep the conversation going by asking her where she'd come from and did she like what she'd seen of Nottingham. Emma gave a deep sigh and stretched out on the carpet.

Gwen put her cup down and went over. 'Her tummy's definitely going down. I certainly think that's working. I'll wait a little longer and see how she is.'

Gwen was beginning to go up a little in my esteem. Perhaps she wasn't so bad after all. Two or three cups of tea later and Don seemed to know everything there was to know about Gwen – where she'd been born, where she'd qualified and why she'd become a vet. I heard most of the conversation second-hand later from Don. I hadn't been listening, I sat watching Emma and praying. Emma sighed again and I went over to her and stroked her. She lifted her head and wagged her tail.

'Look, look! Her tail's wagging,' I cried with great joy. All three of us sat there with silly grins on our faces.

'I'm sure she'll be all right now,' said Gwen, 'but it'll be quite a time before she's herself again. This has obviously been coming on for some time.'

'What about her back legs?' I said. 'Will she be able to walk again?' It seemed as humiliating for a dog to be mentally alert and bodily unable as, of course, it is for human beings. But the thought of Emma becoming an invalid for the rest of her life struck a chord deep inside me. It took me back to my blindness, my helplessness before I had Emma and although now Emma, too, was blind and deaf, those things didn't worry her. She'd adapted marvellously in the house, remembering where all the furniture was, and it was only at times when Kerensa's toys were strewn around the floor or I'd unwittingly moved a chair that I realized Emma couldn't see. Human beings are far more affected by these disabilities than animals. But to lose the use of her back legs – I felt that would be the ultimate humiliation for her.

58

'I think that'll come gradually but you'll have to help her around for quite a while.'

'Why should she go off her back legs if it's something to do with her tummy?' I asked.

'It's so painful,' she explained to me, 'that she tends to hold her muscles tightly and then can't use her back legs. Don't worry, she'll be better soon. I'll come and see her again tomorrow.'

It was two-thirty am when Gwen left our house that Sunday morning, a totally different figure to me than when she had first come in. I had every faith in her now: she was a brilliant vet.

When we returned to the lounge Emma was sleeping peacefully.

'It's a shame to disturb her to take her upstairs,' Don said. 'I don't think it would be good for her to climb the stairs anyway. Shall we leave her down here tonight?'

I reluctantly agreed, knowing it was the best for Emma. But when I entered the bedroom, I didn't dare look at the space where Emma's bed should be. I climbed into bed and closed my eyes to the fact that she wasn't there. I had to keep telling myself that she was asleep in the lounge and she was going to be all right, but I found it almost impossible to sleep in the silence. I was so used to hearing Emma's deep breathing and the occasional little snort and snore from her bed. The silence was overwhelming. I had to try and keep my brain occupied with silly little things ... making shopping lists for the following Monday, mapping out the whole of my day for Sunday – what we were having for dinner, how many potatoes I'd peel, etc. – until eventually I was carried off into an uneasy sleep until the morning.

Emma was still unable to walk unaided that day. We found a long strip of soft towelling which we looped under her tummy to support her as we walked her round the garden.

'The main thing is,' Don told me, practical as always, 'to let her walk around and give her legs a stretch. Don't leave her lying there too long.'

59

I rubbed Emma's back legs constantly and as soon as she looked as if she wanted to go anywhere I helped her up on to her feet, walking her up and down the lounge, round the hall, into the kitchen, out into the back garden. It was at this point that Bracken began to show even more devotion to Emma. He couldn't understand why she had to be helped in and out but it worried him and he would always come with us, walking round her, giving her a lick round the ears and round the nose to reassure her that he was still there.

Emma's recovery from that illness was a slow one, but she did recover and was more and more able to cope with walking on her own. As long as I watched her I could leave her to make her own way up and down the garden. I remember one day I let her out and was watching her rootle around the grass when the telephone rang. When I came back, Bracken was running up and down the hall crying. 'What's the matter?' I asked. He rushed out into the back garden, whining and barking. And there was Emma. She'd fallen over on the grass and had been unable to get up. Bracken was so upset. He ran round her in circles, nuzzling her with his nose, licking her, trying to encourage her to get back on to her feet and then running back and barking at me, as if appealing to me to do something quickly. From that moment on he became her slave – standing over her while she ate her dinner to make sure that Buttons didn't pinch any, escorting her up the garden and back. But it wasn't until Emma was much, much better, when she began to wear her collar and lead again to go for little walks, that Bracken took on yet another role.

CHAPTER EIGHT

BRACKEN HAD FOUND his vocation in life. He changed from a mischievous Labrador into a responsible adult dog and decided he must look after Emma. The first morning that Emma was well enough to go for a short walk, Bracken insisted on coming along too. Buttons wasn't worried as she was still nursing her puppies. As soon as we stepped out of the front door, Bracken took Emma's lead in his mouth. Far be it for me to say that Bracken actually knew Emma couldn't see and that he could guide her – I don't know whether dogs have that much intelligence – but all I know is that he wanted to have the lead and walk her down the drive. He was really thrilled. His tail waved high up in the air and he had a look of total self-sacrifice written all over his face. Emma's pace was that of a snail compared to Bracken but he wasn't worried. He slowed down to suit her. Emma wanted to stop and sniff every piece of grass and every gate-post. Bracken stopped too and sat down, patiently waiting for her.

I've always taught Bracken to sit at kerbs, probably because Emma always did and it was the natural thing for me to do, so, at the first kerb Bracken sat down. Emma didn't. She wasn't very keen on sitting – her back legs weren't pliable enough to keep standing and sitting down at kerbs. Emma carried on, trying to cross the road, but Bracken was most upset about this and sat firm. He turned to look at me with the expression on his face that said, Well, I'm sitting at the kerb. What are we going to do about Emma? But Emma was undaunted, she tried to cross the road. If Bracken hadn't been such a big, heavy dog, I'm sure she would have achieved it. But she didn't. She had to wait until I gave Bracken the okay that all was clear.

Bracken behaved like a true gentleman while he was

taking Emma for her walks. He even ignored other dogs, which, for him, took an awful lot of self-control. A stray mongrel came up and started to show great interest. Bracken gave it a sidelong glance and a low growl but, without further ado, continued to take Emma along the pavement. He had, of late, become very stroppy with strange dogs, especially when he went for his walks in the park. He seemed to be more protective towards me than towards Buttons or Emma, and if any dog came near me he would walk towards it, stiff legged, hackles raised and tail held up in the air. If it refused to go away he made it even more plain by attacking it. This became a big worry to me. I hate to see nasty dogs and although Bracken was completely obedient and would never run off and attack any dog, I still had to be on my guard and try not to let other dogs come near me, which was extremely difficult. I only had to raise my voice to a strange dog to tell it to go away, and that was the cue for Bracken to fly after it to make sure that it did. Of course, he was an entire dog and had already sired a litter of puppies. I had visions of him being a stud dog. His puppies had been so nice and one had been accepted to be a guide dog, but I had to re-think my ideas about this. He was obviously beginning to find his feet as an adult male and I'd got to do something about it. After very careful thought, I took a leaf out of the guide-dogs' book and decided to have him castrated. It worked like a charm. He became even more loving and devoted to all of us as a family, still kept his patrol with Emma up and down the garden and stopped attacking strange dogs. It was a relief to me. I'm surprised how many people think this is cruel because I believe the opposite: that it's cruel to keep an entire dog if you're not going to supply him with bitches. You're asking him to live the life of a monk and, surely, a dog wouldn't choose that life for himself. Bracken still fancies the ladies, of course, but now it's a pleasant chat and a tail-waving session. I would also not hesitate to advise anyone to have their bitch spayed if they have no intention of breeding from her. So many bitches go through a lot of heartache and illness, coming in season time after time without ever being allowed to have a litter of puppies. Many of them have false pregnancies and some of them even produce milk at the right time. Surely this is far more cruel than having a bitch spayed? We should take a lead from some of the Continental countries who charge a higher licence fee for dogs that aren't castrated or spayed. Perhaps that would also cut down the many unwanted puppies there are in England.

The more I know of dogs, the more amazed I become at their differences in character and their variation in intelligence. Even one breed, like Labradors, can be just as varied as human beings, both in their looks and temperament. Mocha was the puppy that made this absolutely plain to me. Mocha is, of course – yes, you've guessed it – another chocolate Labrador. I saw her advertised in one of our dog magazines and I couldn't resist her. Poor Don was just a little perturbed that we suddenly had four dogs but, optimistic as usual, I assured him that sooner or later we'd find a nice house with lots of land and we wouldn't even notice we'd got four dogs then. To this very day, three years after purchasing Mocha as a puppy, I still haven't quite fathomed her temperament out completely. I can't really believe that she's as stupid as she makes out.

The very first day of her arrival, unlike most new puppies who gallop round the garden in delighted excitement, Mocha walked amiably up and down, taking no notice of anything around her, accepting the fact that there were three other big dogs. She appeared to be in a trance-like state as she sat in the middle of the lawn staring contentedly at nothing in particular, while Bracken and Buttons were racing up and down trying to work out what this new puppy was and what it was going to do. Emma, of course, took no notice whatsoever and cleared off to her usual place on the settee in the lounge. But, for all that, Mocha made up for her lack of intelligence with a super nature. I don't think I shall ever meet a kinder, more obedient dog. She just doesn't know how to be disobedient.

Although I don't feel my dogs are human beings, I like to treat them all with respect. This is the way you get the best out of your dog and I can't help seeing human characteristics in them. Mocha reminds me of a little orphan child whenever she sits gazing into the distance with those big, liquid brown eyes of hers. She is transformed in my mind to a little girl of about eight, with red hair and freckled cheeks and one of those big floppy hats which were in fashion before the war, blue ribbons dangling. I imagine her dreaming of what she'll do when she is old enough to leave the orphanage and start a life of her own, of the handsome man she'll meet and marry. And that handsome man, I'm sure, is Bracken. I think it's because I can see now that I read so much into the dogs' expressions and their eyes can make me imagine so many things. If I'd seen all my life, perhaps I wouldn't take notice of this, but eyes are so fascinating. Bracken's show reams of intelligence. I have a picture of him being in the last World War, leading a squadron of fighter-bombers, telling all his many girlfriends that he was winning the war single-handed. He's smart, upright, always joking and a real lady-killer. I can see him in my mind as clearly as I would a close friend, combing his hair in the mirror and laying it down with jars full of Brylcreem and making sure every hair was in place, brushing his uniform down meticulously before going off to lead his squadron into battle. I can also see his last battle over Germany as those impetuous hazel eyes of his dart to and fro while he watches the attackers, and sadly his plane is shot down in flames. This scene is so vivid in my mind that sometimes it really worries me. I wasn't around in the war-time and for me to have the feeling of being in that fighter-bomber with Bracken, and feeling the fear that he did, is very uncanny.

I'm rather glad Buttons doesn't know how I see her, because it really isn't a very nice picture. I get flashes of her wearing curlers and a hairnet, leaning on the garden fence gossiping to anybody that passes rather than doing house-work, always going out on a Saturday night to have a right old booze-up, then returning home to nag a poor, weedy little husband. I had no strange notions about Emma, probably because when I was blind I always thought of her as a person. I always talked to her as we went along the road and I often remember people telling me what a beautiful dog she was. I would stop and think, But I haven't got a dog. Then I'd realize they meant Emma. I am sure this all sounds – even to the most ardent of dog lovers – a lot of sentimental slosh and I hasten to point out that I'm not sentimental about my dogs. They are treated as dogs and they're made to behave themselves and to be obedient, and they are not at all spoilt.

I'm not quite sure if I believe in reincarnation but it's worth thinking about: whether we have to prove our worth before we go to heaven (or the other place for that matter) by coming back as various things – dogs, cats, horses, whatever you like to mention. I'm sure that some of you at one time or another must have looked at an animal and felt it reminded you of someone that you knew. I often get that feeling. Perhaps I should see a psychiatrist.

I learnt such a lot more after having Mocha about the temperament of each dog and how the approach to training had to be so totally different. I had to be very careful about the intonations in my voice when I spoke to Mocha. I couldn't tell her that she was a good girl excitedly. It had to be done very calmly. I learnt this quite early on. If I forgot for a moment and sounded at all excited when talking to her, Mocha would go berserk, leaping up into the air as if she were trying to jump clean over my head. Usually she didn't quite make it and hit me straight in the face. She did this one evening and knocked my front tooth clean out. Luckily it had been capped or I would have been in agony, but I was horrorstruck when I saw my front tooth sailing across the kitchen. Bracken, who had been dozing in the corner, also saw it and leapt up with the speed of light, grabbed it and ate it. I felt such a fool when I arrived at the dentist and told him my tooth had come out and the dog had eaten it, but it wasn't the first time I'd had to tell someone a similar story. Bracken had once eaten one of my contact lenses – not the crunchy type, the soft type – and Kerensa had given it to him. That was after Kerensa had eaten one. I seem to be surrounded by dogs or children that want to eat things. I'm sure there's nothing lacking in their diets.

So placid is Mocha that I can let Kerensa take her on the lead. She doesn't pull, she doesn't bark at other dogs she sees in the streets, and she ignores the ginger toms that sit on the walls though, of course, I wouldn't let Kerensa take her out on her own. The only thing you do have to watch for is Mocha's tendency to walk into things like lamp-posts and walls. Now, Mocha's sight is absolutely perfect, it's just that she doesn't seem to be able to co-ordinate things with her brain – there are occasions when Mocha seems to be alert. I remember one day we were going to the park. Kerensa, as usual, was in charge of Mocha and was walking along the pavement happily singing to herself while Mocha bumped into lamp-posts and brick walls. Suddenly Mocha spotted one of the ginger toms and, for some unknown reason, decided to chase it. I yelled to Kerensa to let go of the lead but no, she wouldn't. I'd always instructed her on how to hold the lead and how to hold on tightly, and no way was she going to let go. Mocha hurled herself and Kerensa into a neighbourhood front lawn and dragged poor Kerensa round some rhododendron bushes. The cat disappeared underneath a gate, which stopped Mocha absolutely dead with a big thud. Kerensa stood up, quite unperturbed, brushed herself down and led Mocha out of the gate, still clutching the lead tightly in her hand.

CHAPTER NINE

IT'S VERY RARE that I go into the surgery to see Don because he's always so busy, and if he gets held up for a minute or so it can leave him behind for the whole day. His patients come in every fifteen minutes or half an hour, so it's only when I have something really exciting which I must tell him straight away that I go in. And this particular evening I'd got something that just wouldn't wait, not even for another three minutes. So I rushed to the surgery, knocked on his door and went in.

'Have you got a minute, petal?' (I always tried not to call him Petal in front of patients, but it's a habit I just can't break.)

'Er, yes. Just a moment.'

I went into the waiting room and looked at the evening paper again. I could hardly believe my eyes.

'Now, what is it? What's so urgent?'

'Look here!' I told him, pointing to a picture in the 'Properties For Sale' columns.

'What's so marvellous about that?' he said after glancing at it.

'It's a kennels for sale. It's not far, is it? Barton Hill, it says. It's just up the road, isn't it?'

'Yes. Let me have a look.' He read the whole advert. 'It sounds just what we want. Have you rung up about it?'

'No, I thought I'd come and show it you first.'

'Well, hurry up and give them a ring. See if we can go and see it tomorrow. I'm not working in the afternoon.'

If I could have driven the car I would have gone there and then, even if only to have a look at it from the outside. It sounded marvellous: '*Kennels for 100 dogs and 80 cats, well established, sold as a going concern.*' But alas, I couldn't see well enough to drive so I had to make do with ringing the estate agents, trying not to sound too excited, and making an appointment to view the following afternoon. There was pouring rain and a howling gale as we turned the corner at the top of Barton Hill to see our kennels but, even in those sort of weather conditions, I knew I wanted it. I knew I wanted to live there, to have as many dogs as I wanted and to be able to run a boarding kennels.

'This is it,' I said as I got out of the car.

'You haven't seen it yet,' said Don, always a little more conservative than I.

'But look at all those fields. I think the property stretches up to that ridge of trees over there.'

'Hmm, quite a size.' Don seemed to be impressed.

Mrs Wood, the owner, greeted us at the door and asked us if we'd rather see the house or the kennels first.

'Kennels!' I said, without hesitation. 'Anyway, we might as well get wet all at once while we're out here.'

She went back inside to fetch some wellington boots and a raincoat. I could tell from one look at her she wasn't what I would call a doggie person. She was too clean-looking for a start. If you're looking after dogs and cats you don't look clean at the end of the day, or even half-way through it. But never mind, I wasn't judging her as a kennel owner. I wanted to buy the place.

'I'll take you through the first block here, where the kitchen is,' she told us. 'The first row of kennels is through here.'

It took me quite a while before my eyes could adjust to the darkness from the kitchen into the kennel block. This is one thing that horrifies me about places for boarding animals. They don't seem to think dogs or cats need to see. So many of them are dark. I had to feel my way along until my eyes became adjusted. The compartments for the dogs were small, not very clean, and in a lot of them I could see cracks in the brickwork. Outside the runs were no better – far too small even for a breed like a dachshund or a corgi. Dogs need exercise, need something to occupy their minds especially when their owners have left them, but they wouldn't get it here. We were greeted by quite a few excited barks, as we went along looking in each kennel, from dogs who were obviously very friendly and were hoping we were taking them out for a walk. Others sat in the corners moping, with sad eyes and longing expressions, thinking, I'm sure, that their owners were never going to reclaim them from this dark prison. My feeling on leaving the kennel blocks was one of terrible depression. And of hope, too, for at least if we did buy this place we'd change it and make the boarders who came to stay with us a lot happier. The cats' accommodation was no better, not in my view. An old shed converted into little pens for cats who could only spend their time stalking around a couple of feet of space.

I tried to make pleasant conversation as I went round, to stop me thinking of how really horrible it was. 'Do you have special feeding times?' I asked.

'Oh yes, about four o'clock we start feeding.'

I looked at my watch. It was four o'clock and some of the cages didn't seem to have feeding bowls in them. Mrs Wood obviously noticed.

'Oh, these cats have only just come in. We never feed dogs and cats for a day or so when they first arrive. It wastes too much food if I do that.'

The thought of leaving either my dogs or cats somewhere they're not going to get fed for a day or two was a shocking thought. The house was better. At least it didn't remind me of prison cells. Not that I was worried about living accommodation at all for I'm sure that once I had the kennels to run I'd only sleep in the house anyway, so I knew that I wanted it. When we got back in the car we sat for a while. Don didn't start up the engine.

'What do you think, petal?' He knew exactly what I thought, I didn't have to voice any opinions.

'Well, at least we can change it,' I told him. 'Make the kennels much bigger by knocking two into one for a start. And build bigger runs on the outside.'

'A good lick of paint would make it look a darn sight

lighter inside,' Don added, rubbing his chin thoughtfully. 'And if we could put some windows inside those kennels, that would make it better.'

We had it all planned. He started the engine and we turned back down Barton Hill. Don hummed carefully to himself. I know that when he hums it means he's thinking hard.

'What is it?' I asked.

'Money!'

'Yes, there is that. Do you think we'll get enough? A mortgage, I mean?'

'They're asking a lot of money for it. We might. We'll keep our fingers crossed anyway. You'll have to do that in the morning as I've got quite a few patients to see. You ring round and have a word with the mortgage companies. Just sound them out a bit, you know, before we start applying anywhere in particular.'

We both knew it was no good going to a building society because they weren't interested in mortgages for businesses, so we had to rely on commercial banks. Sadly, our own local bank wasn't even considering mortgages at that time – or things might have turned out a lot different. That very evening Don started to draw maps of the new kennel blocks he'd build and how he'd change the old ones. He was completely taken up with this new idea and new vocation in life and I was mentally working out how many tins of dog food, cat food and pounds of beef we'd need every week to feed a hundred dogs and eighty cats.

The next morning, at the start of office hours, I sat beside the telephone, the Yellow Pages in my hand, ringing round the commercial bankers. I was lucky for I found one that was interested almost immediately. During the next few weeks we were busy organizing valuations on the kennels, and we had lots of mortgage forms to fill in. Both Don and I were beginning to feel really confident that this was it. I was so confident, in fact, that I decided to splash out and buy Don something really fantastic for his birthday. I didn't like the thought of buying the same old thing for him – aftershave or socks – and he'd always had a yearning for a German shorthaired pointer. They are not at all like Labradors. They're sleek and close coated with long ears, a long nose and no tail, and have the elegance and speed of a gazelle. Don had seen some once at a dog show we'd been to and gazed at them longingly. Then, as if by magic, in the week of his birthday there were some advertised for sale in our local paper. They are a very rare breed so I felt extremely lucky. Teak, as Don called her, was received with great excitement, especially as I'm sure Don thought he was going to get yet another bottle of aftershave or pair of socks.

Teak was to teach me even more about dog behaviour, and about different techniques of training. At eleven weeks old, she looked like a little fawn – all legs and head – as she gambolled round our back garden. The other three dogs were astounded. They knew she wasn't a Labrador and tried to work out what she really was but she was too fast for them and they couldn't catch up with her. Emma couldn't have cared less whether it was a mouse or a baby elephant. Emma was always the same about other dogs: she could take them or leave them. She would always play with them if she found them in the park and they were friendly, but she was never all that keen on making real friends. It was as if she reserved herself for me. She took a sniff at Teak – in one of Teak's fleeting moments as she streaked by – decided she wasn't at all interested and ambled off into the lounge. I always made sure that Emma never felt pushed out and her days were spent wherever she pleased, in the lounge, or hall, or kitchen, but all our other dogs were restricted and they weren't allowed to run through the house in the day. They were either out walking, in the garden or in the dog room. The only time the other dogs were allowed in was in the evening, when Emma had chosen her place to sleep or had gone off to bed upstairs. I also fed Emma separately. Not that the others would have had a chance to steal any of her food (they wouldn't have dared and anyway the meat disappeared from her bowl almost before it touched the ground), but Emma always had to come first. I knew she didn't want to go for

71

long walks, but just a trot down to the local shop with a collar and lead on made all the difference to her day. She loved going to the local shop. There were so many smells and there was always the hope that someone behind the counter would take pity on her and pass her a biscuit or two. I never mind tying any of my other dogs up outside a shop that has a notice 'NO DOGS' but I never did that with Emma. If no dogs were allowed in the shop then neither of us would pass the threshold. But I'm pleased to say our local shop has never needed to put up a notice of this kind and I'm sure the owners have never had any problems with dogs being a nuisance.

Teak immediately tried to assert her authority, for even at that tender age she decided that she was going to be the boss. Once in her bed, no canine was allowed to go near her and she would emit a deep-throated growl of warning that would befit a fully grown great Dane. So far, Bracken had always been boss – after Emma, that is – although Buttons had never admitted it. Mocha was just a born follower, when she remembered who she was following, and both Don and I realized immediately that we'd have to get the upper hand with Teak from the start. Dogs, as far as I can see, fall into two different categories – the leaders and the followers. It goes back to long before they were domesticated and they lived in packs. They always had a pack leader and any dog that wanted leadership had to fight for it. If he won he took over, if he didn't he went back to being a follower. These instincts, I find, are still very prevalent in our domesticated dog. If you have a follower, he's going to be very easy to train, very placid and eager to please. If you have a leader, you've got a totally different dog. I like to think of it this way: the leader dogs are the type that would be good at police work, the follower dogs are the type that would be good as guide-dogs. Buttons and Teak are definitely leaders. We didn't have Buttons until she was a year old, so she was able to form her character before coming to live with us and, of course, a dog with Buttons' temperament felt she had to assert her authority when moving into a new home. She didn't try to assert authority over Emma, but over us. At this point, I must say that a lot of pet owners don't realize what is the basis of their dog's temperament, and they fail to see how they could cure an aggressive dog.

While on the surface Buttons seemed quite friendly to all of us, underneath she was waiting for the opportunity to assert her leadership. It came one night. She was asleep in her basket and it was time for everybody to go out for their last walk. I told Buttons, but she ignored me. 'Come on, Buttons,' I said again. She still ignored me, opening one eye and closing it again. I went up and gave her a pat. 'Come on, Buttons, quickly.' She growled at me. At that point I realized what she was doing. I got hold of her by the scruff of the neck, dragged her out the basket, shook her, shouted at her and told her that she was a very, very bad dog, put her outside and closed the door. If you watch mothers with their puppies, you'll see that they often chastise them by getting hold of them round the neck and shaking them. This doesn't hurt a dog but it seems to humiliate them and certainly puts them in their place. When I opened the door again, Buttons was a changed dog. She'd been reasonably friendly before, but now she was excessively loving. She came round me, wagging her tail, lying on the floor, putting her feet in the air. That is the sign from a dog of total submission. I had won. I often wonder what would have happened if Buttons had gone to someone else who had backed off when she'd growled at them and left her alone. She would have probably taken over and might even have attacked someone.

Teak, being only a very young puppy when she came to us, was very easy to handle and although she growled at the other dogs, she never tried it on with us because she realized from the start that Don and I were the leaders. I always feel sorry for those pet owners who come and tell me what troubles they have with their dogs as, naturally, people do want to discuss their pets with me.

'He won't let me take a bone off him. In fact, he won't let me anywhere near. He growls and I'm sure he'd bite me.'

I tell them that the best thing they can possibly do is to go up and take the bone off the dog. Make a fuss of him. Tell him what a clever dog he is for giving up his bone and give it him back. If he does bite, then bite him back. I don't mean that literally, of course, but to get hold of him and really reprimand him before returning his bone. You may have to do this quite a number of times before the dog realizes that you are the boss. You would be amazed how many dogs are the leaders of their pack and how many dog owners are literally afraid of their dog. I cannot stress enough how important it is that you should train your dog to make sure that he will obey you. I find it much easier to understand now, when I hear that dogs attack people, what's gone wrong. The dog just hasn't been trained to be obedient. Boredom, too, can make a dog aggressive or destructive. Dogs are like children: they need lessons, they need things of interest to do in the daytime. If a child wasn't sent to school at the age of five then he, too, would become bored and probably that old saying, 'The Devil makes work for idle hands' also goes for paws.

CHAPTER TEN

TEAK TURNED OUT to be a totally different kettle of fish from any of the Labradors. When I first took her for a walk in the fields, I let her off the lead and was rather shocked when she had gone in a flash. This had never happened to me before. Labradors just aren't like that. They're not fast enough to disappear in half a second, and they prefer to stay round their owner and keep them in sight. Especially Mocha. I would always be looking for Mocha and she'd be behind me. She never went anywhere. But Teak had gone. What could I do? I couldn't see her anywhere. That didn't mean a lot as I couldn't see far into the distance anyhow. Terror-stricken, I tried calling her back. She was Don's dog: what was I going to do when I went home without her and told him I'd lost her the very first time I had taken her out? Well, how was I to know that she was going to shoot off like a bullet out of a gun? But just as quickly she was back at my feet, leaping up and down with joy. Before I could pat her and tell her what a good girl she was, off she went again. I found this very unnerving at first – one minute Teak would be there beside me, the next she'd be miles away. You need to look into the breed and see what they were originally bred for to find out what sort of temperament your dog is going to have. It is no good expecting a German shorthaired pointer to act like a Labrador, so I had to condition myself to a different breed. Labradors were meant for retrieving pure and simple, they weren't meant to go out and search for birds or point. They were trained to stay behind their master until he gave them the command to retrieve a bird, to go out to it and to come straight back.

The pointer, on the other hand, was bred to range, to range out, flush the birds out and to point. They always like to work a long way away from their owners so I had to accept that Teak's instinct sent her a long way off, but always brought her back. I had hours and hours of pleasure watching Teak. Her movement, her gait, was so different from Labradors. Compared to her gazelle-like gallops they looked like elephants trundling around. She reminds me of a butterfly flitting from place to place with ease and elegance. At her easy canter the Labradors are at a flat-out gallop to try and catch her. They never succeed, not unless she wants them to. Teak's instinct is so strong that all she wants to do when she's out is look for birds or anything that she can chase . . . rabbits, rats, mice. She's so fast that she can almost catch a bird in flight. She hasn't quite caught one yet, just a few tail feathers. She did catch a squirrel in the woods one day and I'm sure would have killed it if it hadn't turned round and given her a sharp bite on her nose.

Out of the two breeds, I must be perfectly honest and say that I favour Labradors. They're very gentle and very affectionate but they don't go to extremes. Teak does. Teak is affectionate, but she is so demonstrative in her affection. She's not happy unless she's sitting on someone's knee, which was fine when she was a puppy but as an adult dog is rather ridiculous. She still insists on her nightly knee-sit with Don.

With five dogs in the house it was more important than ever to have law and order among the pack, as that is what they had become and I felt I was their leader. My weekly visits on a Wednesday night to our local Dog Training Club became even more important to me. Buttons, Mocha and Bracken had all gone to the Beginners' Class and been promoted to the more advanced. The night I turned up with Teak, I was greeted with surprise.

'Good heavens! What's happened to that poor Labrador?' the trainer asked me.

I laughed. 'This isn't a Labrador, it's a German short-haired pointer.' She was surprised. Teak, I hasten to add, is the same colour as the chocolate Labradors, and although it's referred to as 'liver' I much prefer to call her chocolate.

Bracken leading Emma.

At the Pro-Dogs Award. *Left:* Bracken receives the
Pro-Dogs Medal for Devotion to duty on Emma's behalf
from Leslie Scott Ordish, the society's founder. *Above:*
Sheila and Bracken with Barbara Woodhouse and the
other medal-winners.

Emma (lying down) and Bracken with their medals.

The trainer looked at me again . . . and Teak. 'Yes, I see now, she is very different in the face from a Labrador. A German shorthaired pointer – what are you doing with one of those?'

I explained that she was really my husband's dog but I felt I should bring her to the Training Club to get her socialized. If you can get your puppy to obey you in a room full of thirty dogs, then you can get her to obey you anywhere. This is what I call socializing. A dog must get used to meeting strange dogs and strange people. I think I am more aware of socializing a puppy than most pet owners as I realize this is the foundation of training a guide-dog in the puppy-walking period. I have also planned my walks so that my dogs get variety and are accustomed, at an early age, to all the things they might meet in later life. My regular walk in the morning to the park (not the kind with swings and children's play facilities) takes me across a main road and up quite a few side streets where children are playing on the pavement. The main road gets them used to heavy traffic and there are usually a lot of people in the park so they become accustomed to mixing at an early age.

The training of the dogs became quite a challenge to me. I tried to make sure that each time I went to the Training Club my dogs had improved. They'd stay a little longer, they'd do better heel work or I'd teach them to retrieve. Bracken was by far the easiest dog to train and enjoyed working so much that it was a pleasure to take him. Mocha, as I've said before, couldn't be disobedient but I found it hard to teach her new exercises, like the retrieve for instance. She'd fetch the dumb-bell and bring it back to me with pleasure, but that's only if she knew where it was. I tried to teach her to sit and mark where I'd thrown it but I was up against an impossible task: I'd throw the dumb-bell out for Mocha and tell her to fetch it. She'd look at me with those lovely big brown eyes: Of course I'll fetch it. Why don't you throw it first though?

'It's out there, Mocha. Look for it!'

She'd make the effort of going out and searching round a little. It's not there, she'd say. Then she'd lose total interest in what I was teaching her and stand staring into the distance at some mirage that she could see and I couldn't. I decided that as long as Mocha was reasonably obedient, came back to me when called, did all the necessary things – sit, stay and lie down – I was quite happy to leave it at that.

But Bracken was a different matter. Bracken and I were going to go to the obedience shows and we were going to win. I had visions of us in the big ring at Crufts. I might add that to qualify for Crufts with an obedience dog, I would have to win the top honours but I felt sure that Bracken could do this in no time at all. I was very much mistaken.

I should have realized from Emma's attitude to Bracken's obedience training that I was flogging a dead horse. Originally I took Emma with me every week to the Dog Training Club, for despite the fact that she wasn't keen on going I just hated leaving her at home. As the floors at the Club were wooden I always took a blanket for Emma to lie on. The minute I walked into the Club with Emma and one or two of the other dogs a set expression came on to her face and I knew what it meant. What a load of rubbish this is, she'd be saying to herself. I've never seen anything so stupid. People running up and down with their dogs and shouting commands at them. Can't they think of anything better to do with their evenings? She would sit on her blanket and look at the dogs and then back at me, and give a snort. What's it all for? her expression would read plainly. What do they hope to achieve? Why don't they do something useful? Then she'd lie down and close her eyes until the tea-break. Emma never missed a tea-break in her life, at the office or anywhere else for that matter. She would always sit up, bright and alert, waiting for the teacups and biscuits to come round, and although I'd never given Emma tit-bits as a young dog and certainly not to the other dogs in the household, I felt that it was Emma's special treat to have a biscuit or two when she went to the Training Club with me.

Bracken was always looking to Emma for reassurance, and whenever I stood up to take him on to the floor to do one of his exercises he would give her a quick lick as if to say, Sit up and watch me do this, and on return he'd give her the same lick, bouncing round her. Wasn't I clever? What did you think of that retrieve?

Emma was not amused. She would give him a little growl and if he persisted in his bouncing and showing off, she would give a small bark. That's enough, young man, she'd say. You young whippersnappers don't know what work's all about! She'd put her head back down on her blanket with great deliberation and pretend to go to sleep, but I could see her ears flicking backwards and forwards, probably in the hope that there would be a second tea-break before home time.

When Bracken had passed his intermediate test at the Club I decided now was the time to enter for a dog show. There was a local one coming up and Don had promised to take me. The exercises in the beginner class are quite simple: The dog must walk to heel on lead, sitting when the handler stops; then he must do this off the lead; do a recall, where the dog is left in a sit, the handler walks a few yards away and then calls the dog; a retrieve, where the dog must retrieve a dumb-bell and bring it back; and the stays – a sit-stay of a minute and a down-stay of two minutes. That was easy. Bracken loved the stays best of all because, basically, he's very idle.

The Saturday morning of the show dawned with sunshine and blue sky and, as we arrived, I had every confidence that I would be bringing home a large rosette that had 'first' on it. But my conviction began to sink a little as I stood by the ringside watching the other beginner dogs working their rounds. There was something different about some of them, something quite beautiful and stylish in the way they executed the heel work and retrieve. It was so precise and beautiful. I knew Bracken didn't look at all like that. Most of the dogs were Border collies or working sheepdogs, and there weren't many Labradors around. But I stepped into the ring with high hopes.

Now the one thing that I hadn't thought about was my lack of sight, and this created a lot of problems for me. The rings are usually on playing fields or in parks where they're allowed to hold obedience shows and the ring size is roughly ten yards by ten yards, roped off with stakes at the corners. The ropes, to me, are almost impossible to see, they merge in with the grass and unless the stakes are white, I'm lost. I always like to think that I have perfect sight, just like everyone else, or that my lack of sight isn't going to stop me doing anything. That is how I felt when I was blind, though of course it did stop me doing a lot of things. But I didn't acknowledge it then and I still feel the same: I don't want to acknowledge that I can't do anything because of lack of sight. I suppose, if I'm really honest, my sight is extremely limited compared to that of a sighted person. I have a very narrow field of vision and I can't see distance or detail, but I never like to admit defeat. I know that often friends must think I'm rather strange. Sometimes I'll be quite friendly with them and the next time I'll walk straight past them – only because I didn't see them. I don't have a recollection for faces and even if I know what somebody looks like I don't seem to be able to recognize them next time round.

I wasn't going to be defeated this time. I was going to do that obedience test. I stood in the ring, the judge watching, the steward giving commands for right, left, forward, etc. At his command to go forward, I marched briskly off with Bracken, telling him to stay at heel. That was fine.

'Right turn!' the steward shouted.

But I couldn't have turned the right way because I got entangled in the ropes. Bracken sat back and grinned. 'You horrible dog,' I said to him – I knew he was laughing at me. He thought this whole obedience idea was a big joke and now look what a mess I'd got myself into! I was determined to carry on and I did. Despite the fact that Bracken could do beautiful heel work he decided he wasn't going to show how clever he was in the ring and followed a few paces behind me instead of at my side. Every time I stopped and looked at him, he threw his head into the air and gave me a flash of his eyes and a big grin of his teeth. When it came to the retrieve, he'd thought something up for that too. The steward was stood on my right giving me the commands to throw the bell, and the judge was a little further in front of me. Well, it wasn't my fault I hit the judge, she should have moved out of the way faster. Never mind, that would teach her in future. As if to add insult to injury, Bracken rushed out, picked his dumb-bell up and threw it about fifty feet into the air, then he raced round in ever-diminishing circles to see if he could catch it before it hit the ground. He couldn't. It landed in the next ring. But Bracken hadn't read the rule that states, 'Any dog leaving the ring while working would be disqualified'. He shot into the next ring, picked his dumb-bell up and brought it back.

'So much for Bracken being an obedience champion,' I said to the judge on my way out.

'I thought you said he was going to win!' was Don's only comment when I got outside the ring.

'He might have done,' I said, 'but it's just one of his off days.'

Regardless of the fact that I'd made such an awful mess of my first ever obedience show, I was bitten by the bug. I longed to be able to walk into the ring and have a beautifully trained dog at my heels. I was so used to having Emma and having a close relationship with her that I had the need to work with another dog and have the same sort of feeling of partnership between us. That's when I decided that five dogs weren't enough.

CHAPTER ELEVEN

I KNEW DON was going to take a lot of persuading to convince him that a sixth dog was an absolute necessity as far as I was concerned. So, before I started my persuasion, I decided to get a few facts to convince him. And, as luck would have it, the commercial bank we were dealing with for the kennels rang up.

'Ah, your mortgage has been passed by our local branch,' the man informed me.

'That's fantastic,' I said, leaping up and down in excitement and visualizing myself taking over the Barton Hill kennels. 'Can we go ahead straight away?'

'Well, not quite. I'm sure that it will be all right but we just have to get the head office to okay it.'

'Does that create any problems?'

'No, not at all,' he assured me. 'Everything that's passed by the local branch is automatically passed by head office. I don't think you have any worries, Mrs Hocken. It's just a matter of waiting.'

'Thank you!' I put the phone down. Waiting was all I seemed to be doing just lately but, never mind, that was one thing in my favour for another dog. I had all my ammunition ready and one evening when Don seemed to be in a particularly good mood I decided to broach the subject. I'd got all our dogs' pedigrees laid out on the table. 'Have you noticed anything about Labradors' pedigrees?' I said to Don.

'Huh, what's that?'

'Well, look at Bracken's, for instance. It's all show breeding. Look at his grandfather, he was a show champion four generations back. Here we are, look, show champion, show champion. And Mocha's, it's just the same.'

'What about that one down there,' he said, noticing the FT in front of a dog's name. (That means Field Trial Champion.)

'Yes, but that's such a long way back and I'm sure Mocha hasn't got any of that dog's genes in her, aren't you?'

Don smiled, looking at Mocha, who was sitting near the radiator gazing blissfully into nowhere. 'Yes, I don't really think that you're going to be able to train that dog to do much.' He laughed.

'And Buttons,' I said. 'Apart from the fact that she's almost three, she just doesn't have the type of character that you can train for obedience, does she?' Buttons is exceptionally wilful and although I can get her to do as she's told, it takes a lot of doing. I have to be really strong-willed and insist that she does something when I tell her, not when she feels like it. It's a constant battle with Buttons about who is going to win. She'll never accept the fact that it's not going to be her. 'You see, in the obedience ring,' I explained to Don, 'it's not a matter of getting your dog to do what you tell him. I mean, Bracken's quite good at that and he's very intelligent. I've only got to show him something once or twice and he picks it up but he doesn't like the precision.'

Don's eyebrows shot up. 'Precision! What do you mean?'

'Well, the heel work, for instance. He sits when I stop but he won't sit straight no matter how hard I try and then he starts to lose interest if I continue doing it.'

'Don't you think that's your fault?' Don pointed out. I was hoping he wasn't going to say that. I had to admit that some of it must be.

'Yes,' I conceded doubtfully, 'but it's a matter of having the right type of dog for the right sort of work. Now if you want to work in obedience, you must have a dog that's bred for work. I've been asking around and a lot of the obedience people I've spoken to have explained the type of dog you need.'

'They can't all be bred from working stock – that are at obedience shows, I mean,' said Don.

Again, I had to concede. 'No, they're not. But probably the handlers are a lot better than I am.' Perhaps this was the way to get him to understand. 'I need a very easy dog because I don't feel, as yet, I'm a very good trainer. If I could get a nice dog, from a nice working background' (I emphasized the word 'nice'), 'then it would be easy for me and I'd learn a lot more.' Before he could say no, I picked up the advert I'd seen in my *Dog Training Weekly* magazine. It was for black Labradors. The sire, Jasper Boy of Kenstaff, had won one Obedience Challenge Certificate, the highest feat a dog can aim for in the obedience world. And what's more, the ancestors on his side had come from the Guide-Dogs for the Blind Association. 'Sandilands Timber' had been one of their most famous stud dogs and had sired many, many guide-dogs. On the mother's side it was all field trial champions. If I'd have tried to make a pedigree up in my mind of what I really wanted from a Labrador, I couldn't have done better. The speed and working background of the field trial dogs plus the easy nature and kindness of a guide-dog line were absolutely perfect. Don looked at it and he had to admit that the pedigree was beautiful.

'Liverpool,' he said. 'It's a long way.'

'Betty said she'd take me.' I was beginning to get excited.

'Oh, you've asked her, have you?'

'Just in case.'

'Have you rung up about them?'

'Yes,' I admitted.

'And have they got what you want?'

'There's a litter of eight puppies with three bitches in so I'd have my choice if I could go tomorrow.'

'Tomorrow!' For a moment Don was astounded, and then remembering my temperament – if I ever wanted something I wanted it yesterday – he put the paper back down on the table. 'All right then.'

'Thank you, petal. I know we're doing the right thing.' I put my arms round him and kissed him . . . always a fatal mistake when the dogs are around. Teak was in first, trying to climb on to his knee. Mocha was bringing up the rear with Bracken, all trying to get in on the act and the excitement. Buttons was lying in the corner crying softly. That was her way of expressing that she, too, wanted some of the

84

attention. Emma was fast asleep on the settee, oblivious to what I was planning. I rang Betty immediately and arranged that we should set out for Liverpool at nine o'clock the following morning. I could hardly sleep for excitement. This was just what I had always wanted, I told myself. I knew the puppy would be black and I suppose if I'd have had my choice it would have been another chocolate one, but you couldn't have everything. As it was such a long journey, I decided to leave Kerensa at home, thinking she'd get bored.

'Where are you going?' she asked me.

'I'm going to fetch another puppy.'

'Another Emma.'

'Not quite,' I said. 'This one's going to be black.'

'Oh, Mummy, can I have a puppy all of my own?' Kerensa was only three at the time and she dearly loved the dogs and cats, but a puppy of her own, well that was a different matter. I let her share the dogs and cats as much as possible but I feel very strongly about children who are seen pulling dogs and cats about. It's so unfair on the animals.

'When you get older,' I promised her, 'you'll have your own puppy.'

'But I want one now.' She began to cry. '*Please* bring one back for me as well.'

'I'm sorry, Kerensa. I just can't do that.'

'But I want something of my own. You've got lots of dogs and cats and Daddy has. It's not fair.'

Kerensa so loved to participate with the dogs and come out with me when I was walking them, and when I let her hold Mocha on the lead she was so thrilled. But on reaching the park, Mocha's lead had to be clipped on to Kerensa's dress and I had to pretend that she was a dog and walk her round the park on a lead. That was fine, but I don't know what onlookers thought about my taking a child round the park on a lead while the dogs were running free enjoying themselves. It's a wonder I've never been reported to the NSPCC. I picked up Kerensa's stuffed Siamese cat and gave it to her. 'There you are, that's your cat.'

'No, it's not real.' She got hold of it and flung it to the floor.

'Well, you can't have animals if you're going to treat them like that.'

'But I wouldn't. That's not a real one.' She stood thinking for a moment. 'Could I have a rabbit then?'

A rabbit. That was a new one. She had a toy one upstairs which she was very fond of and took to bed with her every night. 'Well, I might think about that,' I told her. 'I'll let you know when I come back.'

She began to jump up and down with excitement. 'A real rabbit, Mummy! Promise! Can I have a real rabbit like Hazel?' (That's what she called her toy rabbit.) I realized I had to make a decision there and then. Children just can't wait.

'All right, I'll buy you a real rabbit if you'll look after it yourself and clean it and feed it and brush it.'

'I will, I will!' She was overjoyed and flung her arms round me and kissed me, as I had done the night before with Don when he told me I could have a puppy. I kissed her goodbye and went off into the car.

I loved going out with Betty driving the car. She's got such a super temperament behind the wheel. She never gets harassed or worried about time and if we get lost – as we often do – we both sit and have a laugh about it before going on our way again. I talked non-stop all the way to Liverpool about my new puppy and how clever she was going to be. It was even more exciting because, apart from Bracken, this was the first puppy I was actually going to choose from a litter, and we didn't really choose Bracken: he was the only chocolate and we didn't have any alternative. So this was my very first choice of a whole litter. I could pick which one I really wanted. I told myself I would be very careful and look at each puppy individually, then watch the litter as a whole before I made my final decision.

Mrs Ward was delighted to see us and she was delighted that one of her puppies would go to be trained for obedience classes, as the father had done so well and mum wasn't doing too badly in the obedience ring either.

'I wasn't sure you'd come when you told me you lived in Nottingham,' she said, as she showed me in. 'Such a lot of people ring up, you know, and don't turn up. I'm sure you'll like the puppies. They're in here, in the kitchen.' She led Betty and me through to a huge farmhouse-type kitchen at the back of the house. 'When people are buying them to train them like you are, I feel happy that they're going to really good homes. I know they're going to be looked after. Here they are.'

There was a big white wooden bed standing in the corner, covered in black puppies. One of them rushed out of the bed, over to me and sat at my feet looking up at me with longing eyes. I picked her up and, as I did so, I noticed the white patch on her chest, exactly the same shape as Emma's. I hugged her to me and she washed my chin. 'This is the one,' I said. 'This is the one I want.'

'You haven't looked at them,' Mrs Ward said. 'There's another seven there.'

'No, this is mine. I don't want to look at the others. I'm going to call her Shadow.'

'Oh, please,' Mrs Ward said. 'I shall be very upset if you don't look at all the puppies before you make your decision. You might have the wrong one there.'

I knew in my heart that this was the dog for me. It clicked the moment I picked her up and the fact that she had a white patch like Emma had obviously got a lot to do with it. But, to satisfy the breeder, I gave her to Betty to hold while I picked each of the other puppies up in turn, but nothing happened with them. Shadow was the one for me. Margaret Evans, the owner of Jasper Boy of Kenstaff, had come along to show me the father and how he worked. He was superb: she showed me his speedy heel work and his wonderful distance control. He had made it to the big ring at Crufts and I wondered if one day Shadow and I would too.

On our journey, Betty had remembered that she had a friend who bred rabbits and felt sure she'd got a litter at the moment. 'I'll take you over on Sunday if you like,' she said, 'and Kerensa can choose one.'

'If we're going to have one, I think we ought to have two – the same sex, of course. We don't want lots of little rabbits about the place, do we?' I have always had this thing about animals living alone. To me it's like a human living all alone and never being able to meet others of his own kind. It seems very cruel. If we were going to have a rabbit, we had to have a pair of them so they'd be company for each other. On reaching home, Kerensa was delighted not only with the new pup but also with the promise that we'd be going to fetch two rabbits the following Sunday.

Shadow seemed to fit into our household like the last piece of a jigsaw puzzle and I was thrilled when she turned out to be just as her name implied, my shadow. She was always there, just like Emma was. But there was a lot of time and hard work in front of me before Shadow would begin to win at her obedience shows.

Six dogs in the house meant a very strict daily routine. Kerensa was now at school in the mornings so that my first job was to get her ready and off to school. Then the cats had to be fed and cleaned and the dogs had to be exercised. It was impossible to take five dogs out at the same time (Emma now had just a small walk a day, if she fancied it, so she went completely separately from the other dogs), and I decided that two and three were easiest to handle. My first walk always begins at half-past nine. I come home for a tea-break and then the second walk begins. When I arrive home again it's time to cook the lunch. There's never a moment free in the day. After lunch I have to answer lots of letters, groom and train the dogs, and then comes feeding time. And evenings are often taken up with Dog Training Clubs. Oh, and of course, I forgot the writing bit. I love writing but I have to try and fit it in between all the other things – usually in the evening when Kerensa has gone to bed. I have bits of manuscript strewn all over the place and can never find them. How I ever manage to do anything amazes me. Being a writer is not like I imagined it would be. I have this picture in my mind of a man sitting in a lonely cottage on a hillside with total peace and quiet, poring over a typewriter. It doesn't work like that for women as there's so much else to do, apart from running the home. And now we had two rabbits to add to the menagerie. Kerensa had chosen a brown one, which she called Hazel, and a white one she named Snowdrop. She was very proud of them and most mornings she was up before Don and I awoke and would be sitting out in the rabbit pen cuddling them and talking to them. I'm not a very nice person in the mornings. It takes me ages to wake up, so when Kerensa comes into my side of the bed and starts to try and wake me, I usually turn the other way, close my eyes even tighter and pretend I haven't heard her. One morning she came into our room. 'Mummy, Mummy, look what I've got.'

I groaned and half opened one eye. One of her hands was clutched round something and I noticed on my bedside table lots of little things, black and round. She picked one up and popped it in her mouth. I closed my eyes again hoping to drift back into sleep and then something started to nudge my mind. What was Kerensa eating? What were those little black round things? I'd seen them somewhere before.

'They're delicious, Mummy.' She poked me again. 'Try one.' She was holding one out to me. I suddenly remembered – I'd seen them in the rabbit run. They were rabbit turds. I shot up in bed. 'Good heavens! Look what Kerensa's eating.' I shook Don immediately. 'Put them down, you silly girl. You'll get all sorts of diseases.'

'But they're lovely, Mummy. I picked them off the bush. Won't you try one?'

As I woke up a little more I realized she'd got a handful of blackcurrants! Don had begun to laugh.

'Oh dear, petal, do you really think she'd do that?'

'Well, you never know,' I said dubiously. Don continued laughing. 'It isn't all that funny,' I said to him.

'No. It just reminded me of that Scottish shop we went to on holiday. Don't you remember?' He laughed again. 'Your sight is a funny thing. You can see so much, but not quite enough.'

I chuckled as I remembered the Scottish shop incident. He was right in one way. My sight did get me into some very narrow scrapes. I'd had to learn to interpret what I actually saw and this was sometimes very difficult, though I'm sure even a sighted person could confuse blackcurrants with rabbit turds – well . . . maybe they could. After years of being blind I'd had to train my brain what to expect and I thought I'd got rather good at it. We were on holiday in Scotland and, looking round the town, Don had spotted a really beautiful tartan shop.

'I wonder if they've got a Hocken kilt,' he said. 'Let's go and have a look.' As the Hockens came from Cornwall and not Scotland, I was sure they wouldn't have, but I, too, was fascinated by the tartan and especially the velvet jackets that were worn by the men. Don left me while he went to talk to one of the assistants about the different names of the clans. There were beautiful models standing about the shop showing the full Scottish regalia and as I still love to go and feel things – I don't get a full picture visually unless I can touch – I went over and felt the sporrans and the kilts, and ran my hand along the black velvet jackets. They were beautiful. One in particular stood out as being really smart. I looked back to see if I could see Don anywhere, and spotted him coming across the shop.

'Come and have a look at this one, isn't it beautiful?' I called. The white lace neck frilled over the black velvet jacket and I stroked the chest lovingly. 'Oh Don, you'd look beautiful in this.' Don looked rather agitated and a little red in the face. 'What's the matter, petal?'

He nodded towards the model. I looked round and it had disappeared. 'I was trying to tell you not to touch that one. It wasn't a model, it was the manager.' I had never felt so stupid before and both of us made a bee-line for the door.

CHAPTER TWELVE

SHADOW WAS ALL I had hoped for. She was perfect to train, so easy and willing to do her work. At five months she passed her test from the Beginners into the Intermediate Class at the Training Club and I couldn't have been more proud of her. She was totally different from the other Labradors, not only in looks but in temperament. Of course she was black, but otherwise she was everything a Labrador shouldn't be for the show ring. Her coat was curly when it should lie flat and thick along the Labrador's back. Her tail was long and feathered. Her legs were slender with little dainty paws. Her face was long with fly-away, collie-type ears. No, if I walked in a show ring with Shadow I was sure they'd all laugh. But her temperament was very quiet-natured and loving; she was eager to be doing things. And how wonderful our home was, enhanced by six dogs of totally different characters.

Despite the fact that Emma was now a very old lady, she ruled over the five with a rod of iron, expecting each and every one of them to stick by the moral standards she had set during her lifetime. Although they would canter around and knock each other over on our walks no one would ever dare touch Emma. But I much preferred to take Emma alone so that we could enjoy our steady walks together. On her good days she would tell me that she fancied just a little walk across the road and up Baulk Lane, where there is an overgrown field on the left, full of fascinating scents. There were times when I would take Bracken too, because he would cry and whine if he saw I was taking Emma on her own. He felt it was his duty to accompany her wherever she wandered. He would tear round her in circles once in the field, looking for pieces of stick or lumps of grass that he could take her as an offering. He would push them gently to the front of her nose as if to say, Come on, play tug-of-war with me. She'd give him a little snort and turn the other way and pretend there was something far more fascinating under that clump of grass. A little daunted, Bracken would place the article on the ground and stand and watch me for a moment before picking it up and trying again.

He would never give up trying to entice Emma to play and sometimes I was quite worried when I saw him tearing up to her with a big log in his mouth, afraid that he wouldn't be able to stop in time, but he always did. It was as if he kept himself in check especially for Emma. As soon as Emma had her fill of the miscellaneous scents she would stand still and wait for me to come and put her lead on again. Reaching home, she would settle in her favourite spot near the television.

In the evenings, when Don and I have finished our work and sit in the lounge, it is total bliss to have the dogs all around us. Emma, who would have had the lounge to herself most of the day, would still be curled up fast asleep in her favourite spot. The other five dogs would first of all, on coming into the lounge in the evenings, pay their homage to Emma, each of them giving her a little nuzzle round the ears and a lick on the face before turning their attention to us. Bracken always comes and sits by my chair and pushes and pushes until I notice him. If I refuse he puts his nose up and gives me a prod under the arm so that my hand falls over his head and he gives me a little nibble on the arm if I stop talking to him or stroking him. Teak comes at me like a cannonball, leaps on my knee, pushes her cold nose all round my ears and leaps off again. Shadow sits quietly by me, just giving me her paw occasionally to remind me she's still there. Buttons will always be lashing her tail on the carpet, crying for attention and then rolling on her back with her feet in the air. Mocha, if she isn't daydreaming, will come up, push with her nose and run off again. It's so pleasant to be there surrounded by all my dogs and I love all the little capers they get up to daily, and the phrase 'the dog ate it' has become a family motto. One day George our gardener popped his head round the kitchen door while I was peeling the potatoes for lunch.

'Excuse me, missis. 'Ave you seen me 'at?'

'No, I don't think so, George. Where did you leave it?'

'Eee, I am sure I left it on that there gate post.' He pointed his thumb back towards the gate. I was so used to George losing things and forgetting where he put them that it didn't really worry me.

'Are you sure you haven't left it in the front, George?'

'I'm sure I left it on that gate,' he muttered to himself. 'Well, I'll go and 'ave another look.' He closed the door behind him.

Don came in a few moments later. 'Have you seen George's hat?'

'No, he's asked me once.'

'Probably didn't bring it with him,' Don said. 'You know what he's like. Have the dogs been out?'

'Yes, I've just let them in again. They're asleep now.'

'They wouldn't have had it, would they?'

'Probably.' I went over to look in the dog room. 'No, it's not in here. No sign of it.'

'I'll go and tell him he's forgotten to bring it with him.' Poor George was sent off on the bus home convinced that he had brought his hat in the morning, while we tried to convince him that he hadn't. It wasn't until that evening I discovered what had really happened.

The dogs were playing in the garden and I heard some unusual growling noises so I went out to have a look what was happening. There was a large hole under the rose bush. Perhaps Bracken had been digging again. Then I saw that all five dogs were round in a circle, writhing and growling and pulling for all they were worth. I didn't recognize it at first, as there wasn't a lot left of it – just the hat band. The hat had disappeared altogether. I knew it was George's. Poor Don was in absolute hysterics as he watched out of his surgery window. 'What are we going to tell George?' he managed to gasp between laughter.

'I don't think we'd better tell him at all, do you?' As the dogs had obviously made such short work of it there wasn't much left to offer George.

'How did they get it?' Don said.

'It certainly wasn't in the dog room when I looked this morning.' I pointed to the hole under the rose bush. 'I would think that Teak found it on top of the gate – she's the only one who could jump that high – picked it up and buried it under the bush until she knew George was safely out of the way, and then unearthed it to play with this afternoon.' Teak loved to jump. She was almost cat-like in her approach to getting what she wanted. She could leap a clean six feet into the air and snatch something that was falling far before any of the other dogs could get it. I would always put food out of the reach of all the dogs but I soon began to realize that, with Teak around, it was no good. She could jump on to the work surfaces in the kitchen without any problem whatsoever and she used her long slender paws like hands to prise open tins, push lids off pans and so on. But all Teak's and the other dogs' antics made life what is was for me, absolutely perfect, until the commercial bank rang me one morning to say that they were very sorry but head office had turned our application down.

'But why?' I asked him. 'You told me that everything would be all right as the local branch had passed it.'

'Yes, I'm sorry. I didn't realize that head office had this policy.'

'What policy?'

'They won't back anything with animals.'

'But why not?'

'I'm sorry, I don't know. They just said that they would definitely not lend money on boarding kennels. I'm awfully sorry, Mrs Hocken, but I'm certain you'll get your mortgage somewhere else.'

I wasn't so sure. Before I had time to collect myself over the next few days from the shock of hearing we weren't going to get our mortgage, I had another blow. Mr Reynolds from the District Council called on me. We had met before over

94

the cattery I wanted to start. My application had been turned down by the council and Mr Reynolds had called then to tell me of this decision. So I wasn't very pleased when I saw him standing there waving a letter in his hand.

'I've received this letter,' he said rather sternly, 'and I'd like to speak to you about it.'

As much as I would have liked to have turned him away, I knew that he was only doing his job and, whatever it was, it wasn't his fault. I invited him in and tried to make him feel at home.

'How can I help you?' I asked.

'Well,' he said, opening his letter, 'we've had a complaint.'

'What about?'

'That you're still boarding cats and that you have some more dogs.'

'Yes, I do have some more dogs,' I assured him, 'but I'm certainly not boarding any cats. I can't, can I? You've refused me permission.'

'I'm only telling you what's in this letter.' He tapped the paper with his hand.

'Would you like to come out and look into the cat houses in the garden? They're all empty, except for my cats, who are out there, of course.'

'I don't mind. If you say you haven't got any boarders . . .'

'No, I haven't, but I insist that you come and have a look.' I had a terrible feeling in the bottom of my stomach at the thought that somebody had complained. Of course, as I've said, we lived in suburbia where not many people seem to like animals, or businesses for that matter. Sometimes I have this awful thought that suburbia – in fact the world – will end up one day without animals in it, without domestic pets, because some bureaucratic body has thought they were a nuisance. I can imagine looking up and seeing no birds in the trees, none flying across the sky, empty parks with no children playing in them because they make a mess, no dogs, no cats. Once we've ravaged the jungles for elephant tusks and leopard skins, we will start on the domestic pets in towns and suburbs.

After showing Mr Reynolds the cattery and convincing him that I'd no cats hidden in boxes anywhere, I introduced him to the dogs. They gave one bark and I told them to be quiet. I have always felt strongly regarding dogs barking. It annoys me, so I'm quite sure it must annoy neighbours and, having six dogs, I felt it was important to keep a very strict control on them all.

'It says in this letter they bark a lot,' he said.

'I don't think so, do you? They're obedient. I don't let them bark.'

'No, I can see that,' he said. He looked a bit further down his paper. 'Well, I don't know whether to mention this or not then.'

'What's that? Not another complaint.'

'Mm, I'm afraid so.'

'What about?'

'About the surgery. They're saying here there's a lot of noise from people walking up and down to the surgery.'

'Goodness me! I never hear them and I live here. My husband is running a chiropody practice,' I said, getting rather annoyed, 'not a daily disco session, you know.'

'Yes, I am sorry, Mrs Hocken. I'm only doing my job. I'm quite happy that everything's in order and I can assure you that if we do get any more complaints, we shall ignore them.' At that, Mr Reynolds left.

We seemed, at that time, to be dogged with bad luck (if you'll forgive the expression). For only two months later our own bank changed its policy and were quite willing to give us a mortgage on any property but, alas, the Barton Hill kennels had been sold. Undaunted, we both continued the search for our Utopia. And, would you believe, the next kennels that we found for sale were withdrawn from the market just as we were about to sign contracts! It sounds very much like a hard luck story, but I don't believe in bad luck, I believe in determination. And anyway, what would we do with our weekends if we weren't searching for houses?

In the meantime, I had my dogs. I put my heart and soul into training them, trying to find out what they really enjoyed doing most of all. Shadow was perfect at the obedience work. What I didn't realize when I decided I wanted to take up obedience showing was that I had to train myself how to walk: I had to be upright, straight, keep the correct pace, turn on the spot. Abouts, left and right turns had to be done with precision, because if they weren't I would lose marks in the ring. I had to remember which foot to use when turning left or right. This is an indication to your dog of what you are going to do. It is no good ambling around and falling over her or it'll put her off doing her close heel work. I had to spend hours not only training Shadow, but training myself. Probably people thought I was absolutely crackers in the park or on the front lawn when they saw me walking round, turning left and right, about turn on my own and counting how many steps I was taking. But, with patience, we both progressed – and how true the saying is that a dog is only as good or as bad as its owner. I know with a better handler Shadow would have got there much faster but I was determined to *be* a better handler and at least I've proved that I can win prizes with her, despite the fact that most of the time in the ring I can't see where I'm going. But determination is what counts. Teak, well she loves jumping and I set up jumps here and there for her so she can have the joy of jumping and I can have the pleasure of watching her. Mocha much prefers to sit and daydream. Bracken I continued training but I was searching for what he liked most of all. I should have known long before I did, for he shares many characteristics with Emma, who loves an audience.

I realized that when I was talking to an audience, Bracken also wanted to be in on the act, and he made it very plain one day when I was addressing a large group of ladies. I had a microphone pinned to the lapel of my suit. Bracken was sitting quietly at my side when suddenly he leapt up in the air, grabbed the microphone off my suit and ran around the hall with it. It had the desired effect, for he received all the attention he wanted. But it wasn't until I met Dorothy Steves that I began to realize what Bracken really wanted to do. He wanted to act.

97

CHAPTER THIRTEEN

I RECEIVED ANOTHER invitation from Shelley Rhodes to appear on the *'Live at Two'* programme for Granada, and what a very different kettle of fish this programme was going to turn out to be – a particularly doggy one. All kinds of people had been invited to appear with their dogs. I decided, of course, to take Bracken. It was a programme made to show the public what dogs could do. People who worked at Granada came along with their different types of pet dogs, and a nearby Dog Training Club brought their team who put on displays to raise money for charity. Britain's top working sheepdog was there, plus many more. It was only the day before that I received a call from Granada to ask me what Bracken could do.

'What do you mean, what can he do?' I asked.

'Most of the dogs that are appearing on the programme,' Lynn, the programme researcher, informed me, 'are going to *do* something.'

'Why didn't you tell me that before? Am I expected to do something with Bracken?'

'It was just a thought,' she told me. 'Can he do anything?'

The one thing Bracken really enjoyed doing was retrieving, so I thought maybe he could do some scent work by finding my article from among other people's. I promised Lynn that I would produce something out of the hat for the next day, hoping that Bracken would be in the mood to do it. Betty was the one elected to take me up to Manchester, as Don was rather busy, and we got lost as usual. We passed Oldham Post Office three times, but we arrived eventually. When we were shown into the Hospitality Room, Bracken was absolutely astounded. He'd been in lots of television stations and knew he was going to enjoy himself but he'd never been in one where there were thirty dogs in one room. He stood rooted to the spot by the door, looking around at dogs under tables, dogs on knees, dogs barking, and then stared back at me in total astonishment. His expression gave away his thoughts: Now this is what I call a television studio, he was saying. Being an old hand at this kind of thing he felt that it was up to him to show the other dogs how a television personality should behave, so he was on his very best behaviour. He walked calmly down the room, ignoring all the dogs that were leaping out to sniff him, and sat by my chair looking positively angelic.

This was a live show and both the director and Shelley Rhodes, I felt sure, thought it might be rather hectic, so we were all asked to be there early and lunch was provided for us. We were all given the chance to go through our particular part. There was only one thing that was worrying me and that was my tooth. Mocha had done it again: the night before, I'd been too enthusiastic when I told her what a good girl she was and she leapt straight up in the air on one of her Olympic high jumps and hit me in the face. I managed to save the tooth she knocked out and stuck it back in, but I hadn't had time to go to the dentist. I'd rummaged in the kitchen drawer for some glue we had, scrutinized it very carefully to make sure it didn't say anything about being toxic and stuck my tooth in with it. I'd been absolutely sure that morning to put the tube of glue in my bag in case my tooth fell out again, and it did. We were provided with a salad lunch with prawns and my tooth fell out right in the middle of my heap of prawns. Luckily for me, Betty was sitting next to me.

'Betty,' I whispered, hoping that nobody else had seen what happened. 'My tooth's fallen out and I can't find it anywhere.'

She scratched around my plate with a fork until she found it. 'There it is,' she said.

I grabbed it and rushed off to the ladies' loo to stick it back in again. I didn't dare eat any more lunch and prayed it wouldn't fall out in the middle of my interview. Then Dorothy

Steves came and sat next to me, introduced to me by Peter, the producer. I'd heard of Dorothy. She trained dogs for films and had a very famous dog in the past called Radar, a most notable four-legged film star. He was a German shepherd who, in his day, was probably more famous than any Hollywood actor. Poor Dorothy had hardly had time to get herself seated when Peter dropped his bombshell.

'Now then, Dorothy. I particularly asked you to come up to train one of these dogs. You've got quite a choice, there's about thirty here.' He waved a hand round to indicate the many dogs. 'Could you train one to do something that you would do in a film, say, just to show the public how you work?'

I could see the look of horror on Dorothy's face. 'You mean you want me to get one of these dogs trained for the programme?'

'Well, yes, of course. You can do that, can't you? You do train other people's dogs for roles in films.'

Dorothy nodded, speechless.

'How about my poodle?' Peter said. 'He's over there, look.'

I glanced over to a sweet little apricot poodle who was standing on his hind legs, waving his front paws madly in the air, trying to get to all the bitches in the room.

'How old is he?' Dorothy asked.

'He's seven I think, but he's a charming little dog,' Peter assured her. 'I'm sure you could train him.'

'But it doesn't work like that. I just can't train a dog in a few minutes to do something.'

Peter looked at his watch. 'You've got two hours. The programme doesn't start until two o'clock.'

'You can't train a dog for two hours solidly,' Dorothy explained. 'You can only teach them for a minute or two at a time otherwise they get bored, and I have to have the type of dog that I can work with.' I could see she was beginning to feel desperate, for it was rather a lot to ask.

'I'll leave it with you,' he said with great confidence. 'Look around the room, you can have any dog you like.' He went off expecting miracles.

All this time, Bracken had been sitting gazing at Dorothy with loving eyes, pushing her hand occasionally with his nose. I have met many dog trainers but none like Dorothy Steves. Her attitude towards dogs was completely different. She was calm, quiet and reassuring. No sergeant-major bellowing. And I knew by her attitude that she could weigh a dog's temperament up within minutes.

'You can have Bracken,' I told her. 'He's quite used to obedience training and he likes you. I'm sure he'd do anything for you.' Dorothy was fondling one of his ears and looking down into his face.

'That is kind of you. I do think that he would work for me and perhaps I could teach him to do just a little something within the time. Do you mind if I just go and take him for a walk before I make my decision?'

'No, fine.' I handed over his lead. There are very, very few people that I would let take Bracken for a walk, let alone entrust them with training him, but I had a feeling about Dorothy and I knew that her methods of training would be persuasive, not forceful. Within a minute or two they were both back, Dorothy smiling, Bracken wagging his tail with a look of eager enthusiasm about his face.

'Yes, I'm sure we're going to get on. What I'll do, if you don't mind, is keep taking him away, just for a couple of minutes, and bring him back to you for a rest.' I had no idea what Dorothy was teaching him to do or whether he was responding to her, but every time she appeared and took his lead from me he wagged his tail and went off with her with great eagerness, so I knew she was using the right approach as far as Bracken was concerned.

Betty had also been talked into taking part in the programme. She was given the producer's poodle: they were having a little quiz to start with for the audience – six dogs, six owners and they had to match the dogs with the right owners. Betty was dragged in to be a handler and she was given the poodle.

'What do you have to do?' I asked her.

'Nothing much. I just have to sit there with the poodle

until the owner comes for him. When they've done the competition they're going to show six owners and then six of us handlers with the dogs.'

'That should be fun,' I said. I love matching dogs to owners. It was five minutes to *ON AIR* time and the studio was crowded. The audience had been invited to bring along their own pet dogs and I think there were more dogs than people. I had to do my interview first, then hand Bracken over to Dorothy and, as she was now showing Bracken working, I decided not to do his retrieving act.

The first part of the programme was the quiz. I watched Betty with her little apricot poodle, while the cameras scanned the dogs, the handlers and the owners. Betty had bitten off rather more than she could chew by offering to hold the poodle as he continually tried to mate dogs either side of him and cried if Betty thwarted his efforts.

'Can't you keep that poodle still?' one of the cameramen asked her. There was no sound coming on at this point, it was wild tracked with music. 'Will you stop him mating with that bearded collie! It doesn't look very nice, does it?'

Betty was flanked on one side by a bearded collie and on the other by a large, friendly Irish wolfhound – not the type of dog suited to a toy poodle, but that didn't seem to daunt him at all. I was astounded at Bracken's good behaviour. Not only was he surrounded by dogs he'd never met before, but by ducks as well. The sheepdog that had been brought in was demonstrating herding, but as the studio was far too small to hold a flock of sheep some ducks were brought in for her instead. Bracken was fascinated by them and lay, ears pricked, watching every movement. My interview over, I handed Bracken over to Dorothy and went to sit at the back of the studio so as not to disturb him. He sat by her side looking up at her with a strange look in his eyes and I was beginning to wonder whether he would do the work. But, as soon as she asked him if he was going to show the audience what he'd learnt, a kind, warm expression came into those lovely eyes of his and his ears came forward, waiting. She took him off the lead, told him to wait and walked across the studio. Then she beckoned to him.

'Come slowly,' she encouraged. She was demonstrating how he would take the part in a film of a very sad dog. Each paw he put down on the floor very carefully. Very slowly he moved towards her. She patted her hand on the floor and he lay down. 'Put your head on your paws,' she encouraged him quietly. Bracken looked around the studio weighing up the audience, perhaps looking for me. My heart began to pound. Was he going to do it?

'Put your head down on your paws,' she asked him again quietly, and he did, very sadly. He lay there, head on paws. He looked so sad I found myself believing him and tears were stinging my eyes. The audience broke into spontaneous applause and Bracken jumped up in the air, wagging his tail, as if to say, well, I was only acting. I'm not at all miserable really.

I found it incredible that Dorothy had taught him to do such a convincing act within a matter of minutes and that she'd used no force, no loud voice. She had just asked him kindly if he would co-operate. It also left a very deep impression on me that Bracken had enjoyed doing his act so much and, after reading Dorothy's most moving book about Radar, I realized that there were lots of things I could teach Bracken to do.

Radar had been one of those very rare dogs who would do anything Dorothy asked him. His fame over here was mainly in *Softly Softly*, the police series on television. Radar could answer the telephone, chase and apprehend a criminal, save a baby from a burning building – to mention just a few of his feats. And it became a challenge to me to see if Bracken would be capable of doing any of these things, not for film work because Dorothy is always the expert on that, but just because Bracken enjoyed learning. And, almost immediately, he was given the opportunity to prove whether he could act or not.

CHAPTER FOURTEEN

I WAS APPROACHED by a French television company who asked if I'd be interested in doing a short piece of film for a documentary programme. I agreed on the condition that if they wanted to film Emma, it would only be for a short period and I was the one to say when she'd had enough. She was an old lady by then and I needed to protect her from these things. If I wasn't careful, Emma would be dragged all over the place just for people to see or film her. She'd deserved her retirement, so I only let people photograph her or film her if I felt she wanted to do it.

It was snowing heaven's hardest when the first two of the French crew arrived: Jacqueline and Jean. They could only speak very little English but I managed to understand who they were. Jacqueline was the programme researcher, Jean the producer. I realized, with a sinking heart, how difficult my day was going to be when Jacqueline managed to tell me that none of the crew that were arriving later could speak English at all.

'In fact,' she told me, 'they should have been here to meet us now. I think they are lost.'

'Where are they coming from?' I asked. 'Why weren't they with you?'

'Some sort of slip-up in the arrangement. We came to Birmingham Airport and they arrived in at Manchester.'

'But Manchester's miles away,' I told her. 'Why didn't they come to Birmingham too?'

'We didn't realize which would be nearer,' she explained, 'not knowing where Nottingham was. And also, I'm afraid we haven't got a hotel.'

I was horrified. The thought of going into a strange country, not knowing where to go and not even having a hotel booked would have worried me, but they didn't seem to mind. It wasn't difficult to find them a local hotel, but what *was* difficult was explaining how they were going to get there. I found the best answer was to put everything down on paper, so I drew them a map.

'I think we'd better wait a little while,' said Jean, 'for the other members of our crew.' They waited, and waited, and evening drew in. Eventually they decided they must go to book in at the hotel, leaving me with the very dubious task of explaining to four French-speaking crew what had happened.

They arrived at about eight o'clock. They had, of course, got lost from Manchester and it had taken them nearly all day to find Nottingham. I ushered the four of them into the lounge and gave them hot drinks. I couldn't believe that none of them could actually speak English, so I stood in the middle of the room and looked round. 'Are you sure none of you can speak English?' I said. They all stopped drinking, looked up at me and grinned. 'Well, it's no good because I can't speak any French and how am I going to tell you what's happened to Jean and Jacqueline?'

'Ah, Jean et Jacqueline,' they repeated.

'Yes, that's right. They've gone to their hotel.'

'Hotel?' one of them said brightly.

'Yes and you must go to your hotel, otherwise the reservation on your rooms will be cancelled.' They all sat there grinning at me. One of them, a huge man well over six feet, with enormous feet I'd never seen the like of before (afterwards I found out he was the cameraman), stood up and went to the front door. I had to stop him – I couldn't let them go out. I ran to the front door and put my arms out over it. 'No, no. You must wait. My husband will take you to the hotel when he's finished his surgery, but you must wait.'

He threw his hands apart and talked a lot of French at me. I took hold of his arm and managed to drag him back into the lounge. We had decided, Don and I, that it was far easier for him to take them round to the hotel than trying to explain and let them get lost yet again. I had to wait a whole hour before Don had finished in the surgery and the time was spent with me monotonously filling their cups with tea and coffee. It ended up with us all sitting round in the lounge and every time I looked at one of them or moved, they all gave me a big grin. This reduced me to hysterical laughter and then they all started laughing. When Don came in, he stood at the door looking round in astonishment.

'What's so funny?' he asked me.

'I don't know,' I said, wiping the tears from my eyes. 'And they don't either.'

All six of them arrived promptly at eight-thirty the following morning to start our day of filming. The snow was still thick on the ground and I was a little worried about Emma's part in the proceedings. I tried to make Jacqui understand that if Emma didn't like the snow or was tired then we'd have to give up filming. Jean was relying on me to show him where the best place to film was and I walked up the lane opposite our house to the field, trying to demonstrate that Emma and Bracken would walk up there and back, Bracken leading Emma with her lead in his mouth. Once I felt Jean understood, I fetched Bracken and Emma. Emma was thrilled with the snow. Despite the fact that she was sixteen, she still revelled in it.

'Okay,' I shouted to Jean who was waiting at the bottom of the drive, camera and sound-men positioned, 'we're ready to start!' Nothing happened. 'We're ready when you are!' I tried again. Still nothing happened.

Jean came walking up the drive. 'We are ready?' he asked in broken English.

'I've been trying to tell you that,' I explained. I realized the day was going to be fraught with language difficulties, but Emma's piece of filming, luckily, went smoothly. Bracken took her up the lane to the field and back again without any technical hitches. Then we had a lot of mock-up filming without Emma. Jacqueline described to me what Jean required: a picture from Emma's eye view of Bracken leading her, which meant Bracken walking from the field down the lane to the main road, with the camera behind him at Emma's eye level. Jean positioned the cameraman – the huge man with dark curly hair and big feet – behind Bracken, with the heavy camera on his shoulder. He was so big, he almost had to crawl along the ground to get Emma's view. He secured the end of Bracken's lead round his wrist and all was ready. Don had come out to help with the filming in his lunch-break. We were told to stand at the bottom of Baulk Lane, which was quite a steep hill, and call Bracken to us when we were given the signal by Jean.

'It will be better if I whistle to him,' Don said.

'Can you move round the corner out of sight?' Jean called. 'Hide behind that hedge. We don't want to mess the shot up with you in it, do we?'

Don and I moved round the big hedge at the bottom. Don took his whistle out and gave it a short blast. We stood there for quite some time listening.

'I can't hear him coming. Do you think he's heard the whistle?' and he gave another sharp blast. This was followed by quite a lot of cries in French, a brown *w-who-osh* and some, what I assume, was French bad language. Bracken had heard the first whistle and had come trotting quite nicely down the hill. On the second whistle he had felt the urgency of it and changed immediately into a gallop, only stopping at the bottom when he spotted us. The poor cameraman, unable to unloose Bracken's lead from his wrist, had been dragged down the hill at full speed. His first thought had been to save the valuable camera, which he managed to hoist further on to his back. As Bracken stopped the cameraman was hurled round like a jack-knifing articulated lorry and smashed into the oak tree at the bottom. Bracken stood, still attached to the cursing cameraman, grinning, tail wagging and his ears in that 'rose petal' position. 'Wasn't that clever? I enjoyed doing that!'

The scene was shot eventually (after the cameraman had been revived with a tot of whisky) with me walking behind Bracken to tell him to walk steadily. Then came Bracken's chance to prove himself as an actor. Jacqueline was explaining to me that it would be really nice if they had a picture of Emma as a guide-dog, showing how she took me about to find bus stops and so on.

'But that's impossible,' I told her. 'Emma doesn't work any more. She can't even see where she's going.'

'Yes, I understand that but Jean feels we need the comparison.'

I sat down and thought for a moment. 'What about Bracken? He could play Emma's part. That is, of course, if you keep the camera off his back end so nobody realizes he's a dog.'

'I'm sure we can do that. Have you trained him to be a guide-dog?' Jacqueline asked.

'No I haven't, but let's see what happens.' I took Emma's old harness down from the coat stand and put it on Bracken. He was quite unperturbed and sat there like a veteran guide-dog. 'Well, so far so good,' I told them. 'Let's try it. There's a bus stop up the road. Would you like me to walk from here to the bus stop with him?'

'That would be fine,' Jacqueline nodded.

I didn't know how I was going to get Bracken to look as if he were guiding me, or how he could understand what I wanted from him. He had never heard of a bus stop, nor had he any guide-dog experience. He walked down the drive in front of me, looking quite important with the white harness on his back.

'Straight on, Bracken,' I told him. I knew I'd have no problems at the kerb because he always sat. 'I want to go to the bus stop,' I told him as we walked across the road. For some unknown reason, he didn't put his nose down and sniff, he walked amiably in front of me, keeping the right tension on the harness, looking just as if he were a real live guide-dog. 'The bus stop,' I told him again as we reached the next kerb. He glanced back at me with a knowing expression and then walked along the pavement straight to the bus stop and sat down. To the crew it was just another shot in the can. To me it was almost a miracle. How did he know? How could he know? But he'd done it. He'd proved himself to be an actor.

Kerensa with Mocha, who is half asleep as usual.

Above: Shadow. *Top right:* Shadow doing an obedience
test. *Below right:* Shadow and Teak.

Buttons' puppy, now carrying on Emma's work as a
guide-dog.

We finished the outside shots just as the light was going. We then had to do all the inside shots. I never, ever want to make a film or be a film star – it's too much like hard work.

'I want some shots of breakfast time,' Jean announced. 'This is morning, no?'

'No,' I said to him. 'It isn't.'

'You don't understand,' he told me. 'This is morning for the film.'

'Ah, I see. Just for the film, I will pretend it's morning.'

The kitchen was commandeered for the next scene, cameras, lights and sound. There was hardly enough room for us to move. It was planned that Don should come into the kitchen for his breakfast and I should carry a glass of milk with a plate of cobs over to one of the work surfaces. The entrance that Don was elected to come in was from the dog room.

'You have just come down,' Jean told him, 'for your breakfast. You go over and kiss your wife. You understand?' Don understood. But I was unable to close my mind to the fact that Don was emerging from the dog room supposedly after a night's sleep. To me that was hilarious and every time I tried to look serious and carry over the plate of cobs I began to laugh and all the cobs fell off the plate. Jean, who didn't see the funny side of it at all, was tearing his hair out after half an hour of trying to get a minute of film.

I never actually saw the finished product as it was only put out on French television, but I heard from Jacqueline that all went well and people were fooled into actually thinking that Bracken was Emma in her earlier days.

CHAPTER FIFTEEN

'PRO-DOGS RANG tonight,' Don told me as soon as I came in the door. I'd been to my Dog Training classes.

'Oh, what did they want?'

'Something about awarding Emma a medal. I'm not sure. Anyway, he's going to ring you back. It was a Mr Imber.'

Pro-Dogs is a public relations organization for dogs, set up in 1976 to help educate the dog-owning public on how to look after their dogs and to become better owners. Their motto is Education not Legislation. It is far easier to educate people on where and how to exercise their dogs than have a local council legislate and ban them from public areas, as is happening all over the country at this moment. Each year a small number of dogs are chosen to receive a medal for outstanding work and I become very excited at the prospect of Emma being nominated for one of these medals. I had only just hung Bracken's lead up when the phone rang again. It was Brian Imber.

'Mrs Hocken, I would like to inform you that Emma's name has been put forward to receive the Devotion to Duty Gold Medal of the Year Award.'

'That's marvellous!' I said to him. 'What an honour. I'd be delighted to accept for her.'

'The presentations are in London, preceded by a dinner. I hope you'll be able to come – and bring Emma, of course,' he added.

For a moment, I wasn't quite sure what to say. I knew that under no circumstances could I undertake a trip with Emma to London. She was far too old to be bothered with a long journey. 'I'm sorry, I won't be able to do that,' I told him. 'Bring Emma, I mean. I don't take Emma anywhere with me now. She much prefers to stop at home. I take Bracken instead. I'll bring him with pleasure.'

'Oh dear, I'm afraid that throws a different light on it, Mrs Hocken. We do have a policy, you see, that all the dogs who receive the medals should be there in person.' I could say nothing. 'I'm sure you understand, Mrs Hocken, that we can't very well present medals to dogs that aren't there. It would be a bit silly, wouldn't it?'

I agreed with him but re-stated that I could take Bracken on Emma's behalf and would be very pleased to do so.

'I will put it to the committee,' Mr Imber told me very uncertainly, 'and I'll let you know.' He put the phone down.

I walked into the lounge and sat down on the settee.

'Well?' Don asked. 'Is Emma going to get a gold medal?'

'No, she isn't.'

'Why not?'

'He told me that unless Emma could be there to receive it herself, it was very unlikely that she would receive the medal.'

'But didn't you explain that Emma was too old to travel all that way?'

'Yes. I offered to take Bracken in her place but he didn't sound very interested. Oh, he said he'd put it to the committee, but you know what it's like. They want the dogs to actually be there. I can't blame them.' But I felt terribly hurt inside, especially as, to me, Emma of all dogs deserved recognition for the years and years she spent as my eyes and the many hearts she had won over since she had retired. And, as hard as I tried, I couldn't push the thought of Pro-Dogs out of my mind over the next few weeks. Emma was being denied her recognition because she had retired and was too frail to travel to London to receive her medal for herself.

I had managed to convince myself that I would never hear from Pro-Dogs or Brian Imber again, when I received another call from him.

'Hello, Mrs Hocken. I'm very pleased to be able to tell you that Emma has got the Gold Medal and we would be very grateful if you would bring Bracken to receive it for her.'

I was astonished. 'But I thought you said they wouldn't award it if she didn't come.'

'No, no, I didn't say that at all. I said that up to now it had been Pro-Dogs' policy only to award the medals to dogs who would come and receive them, but there's always an exception to the rule and all the committee and I agree that, regardless of whether Emma will be there in person or not, she deserves the medal for her devotion to duty.'

The dinner and presentation is the most cherished occasion in my life so far and also the most emotional. There were two car loads of people travelling down from Nottingham on that cold December day and lots of friends from London had also bought tickets to come and share my most memorable day. The Grosvenor Rooms, where the celebration was to be held, was buzzing, alive with people and cameras and, as I stepped into the large ballroom with Bracken, the cameras began flashing. My heart ached for Emma – for the first time in many years I felt desperately alone without her, and if Don and so many of my friends hadn't been around me, I might have turned tail and run.

When I was blind I had a recurring dream that haunted me: that I was in a city alone – without Emma, I mean. There were lots of people around me and I could hear the traffic zooming past but I hadn't got Emma and had no means of safely getting away. I'd always wake up in a cold sweat and feel around the bottom of the bed to make sure Emma was still sleeping peacefully before I dared go back to sleep again. And that's how I felt at that moment. The evening was made even more difficult for me because everyone who came up to talk to Bracken assumed he was Emma and I had to go through the painful explanation of why she hadn't accompanied me. But then I am thankful for having someone like Bracken, who is, himself, a very special dog. He has an uncanny way of knowing what's expected of him. Before the presentations I was asked to do a short piece of film for the television news and, while I was being interviewed, Bracken, rather than lying on the floor out of camera shot, put his two front paws on my knee, looked at the camera and gave me a nudge with his nose, reassuring me that he wouldn't let me down. We had built up a very close relationship, enhanced by the fact that I had realized what Bracken enjoyed doing and had taught him many things over the last month or two. Now he would pick up the telephone when it rang and hand it over to me, he could count by barking, lick his lips or grin on my command and, most amazing of all, I had taught him to chase and attack a criminal. It was quite strange to see Bracken, the gentlest, sweetest natured dog I know, chasing and grabbing someone's arm, not letting go and growling ferociously. He made it look very convincing.

I don't think anyone realized how much courage I needed to go up on that stage in front of all those people and cameras to receive the Gold Medal without Emma by my side. I stood on stage, alongside the other recipients of the medals, while the speeches were being made. The whole atmosphere was electric with emotion. I forced myself to concentrate on what was happening. Barbara Woodhouse was receiving an award for outstanding contributions to responsible dog ownership. Her speech was magnificent. Like a lot of clever people, Barbara Woodhouse had a charisma about her that held the whole room spellbound.

'Our next award,' the compère continued, 'goes to Dougal for Life Saving.' Dougal was a little Pekinese who had saved his owner, Mrs Sheldon, and her daughter from certain death, when their flat had been filled by poisonous carbon monoxide fumes caused by a block in a flue. The two occupants had collapsed unconscious in the kitchen and Dougal had persisted in trying to wake them up by scratching and licking their faces and nuzzling at them until Mrs Sheldon came round enough to crawl out and get help. 'Another few minutes,' the hospital told them, 'and you would both have been dead.'

I was awe-inspired to think that such a tiny little dog could save the lives of two human beings.

Kalli was the next to receive her award. A little cross-bred collie who lives with her owner, Mrs Symington, at the Guisborough Grange Bird and Pet Park. Kalli was purchased from a pet shop for the sum of three pounds and had turned out to be worth her weight in gold. She had fostered many of the orphan babies that Mrs Symington had taken in, including Arctic foxes, pumas, lions and tigers.

'The Devotion to Duty medal is awarded to Emma,' I heard the compère saying. He told the audience of some of the things that Emma had done for me as a guide-dog and explained why she couldn't be there in person and that Bracken was her stand-in. I watched the compère place the medal around Bracken's neck and take the few steps towards me, holding the microphone out, hoping I, too, was going to say a few words. I was too overcome to be able to tell the audience how much Emma meant to me. I could feel my body shaking all over, my nails dug into the palms of my hands and I bit my bottom lip and closed my eyes tightly to try to gain control of my emotions, to fight back the reality that Emma was an old lady and it was Bracken on the other end of the lead. She should have been there to share in our moment of triumph. I looked at Bracken, who sat with all the poise and dignity of a young Labrador, and envied his youth on Emma's behalf. As much as I loved Bracken and all my dogs, no one could ever take Emma's place.

When the presentations were over, I found I was able to relax and enjoy my evening. It was wonderful to be in a room with two hundred or more people whose greatest joy in life was their dogs, and there were so many people I wanted to talk to. I had read many of Barbara Woodhouse's books and seen her dog-training programmes on the television, and I wanted to express my personal thanks to her for the good work she had done over the years in bringing the ordinary dog owner's attention to the fact that dogs need training. And, being an author myself, I know how nice it is when people come up and tell me they've enjoyed my books.

'Can you see Barbara anywhere?' I asked Deirdre. (Deirdre and John, being dog lovers, had jumped at the opportunity to come to the Pro-Dogs evening with us.) The room was crowded with people and it was difficult for me to sort out who was who. I still find using my sight takes quite a bit of concentration and to recognize people's faces among so many is a difficult task that I'd rather leave to a fully sighted person.

'Follow me,' Deirdre said, pushing her way through the crowd. She took hold of Bracken's lead so that I could just concentrate on following her. We introduced ourselves to Barbara, who was busy answering questions from hundreds of admirers. She instinctively reached a hand out to stroke Bracken while she was talking to us. At that point she had my greatest sympathy, for I knew what it was like to be in the limelight and to remember to smile at everyone and I hope that when I reach her age I shall have as much energy and enthusiasm as she has. I suddenly felt empty-handed and realized that I hadn't got Bracken's lead in my hand and reached across to take it from Deirdre. I didn't realize that she had it tightly wrapped around the wrist of the hand that was holding a full glass of champagne. Without thinking, I gave a little tug on the lead. At which point Deirdre threw her glass of champagne all over Barbara! I wasn't sure whether to laugh or to disappear into the crowds, but I should have known that nothing daunts her. She laughed with us and, always finding the right remark for the right occasion, told us she felt she'd just been launched.

I then went to seek out Dougal and Kalli, for I wanted to meet those very special dogs in person. Kalli was the typical black-and-brown mongrel dog you see roaming the streets of our cities any day but she'd had the good fortune to find the right people and the right vocation in life. I had to take my turn along with many others to have a cuddle of the brave little Dougal. Bracken, who'd never met a Pekinese before, wasn't quite sure what to make of him, especially when I picked Dougal up and held him in my arms. He sat with a perplexed expression on his face, head cocked to one side with that 'protection' look in his eyes. Whenever I am approached by another dog or I go up to make a fuss of someone else's dog, Bracken is always there, standing over me like a big, brown guard, in case anything goes wrong.

'He's a dog, Bracken,' I explained, kneeling on the floor so that Dougal and Bracken were on the same level. Bracken was intrigued. He nuzzled through his fur, found his ears and his nose, gave his face a friendly lick and accepted him for what he was.

I felt a very deep link with Kalli and Dougal's owners – a feeling I knew well, of owning a dog who was very, very special.

CHAPTER SIXTEEN

NINETEEN EIGHTY-ONE did have its good days, but they were completely blacked out for me by the horror that I had to face between May and November. It began with Shadow. We'd been working so well together and I had been looking foward all winter to the start of the obedience show season in March. As early as the beginning of February I had begun to plan our first show, even down to what I was going to wear and what sort of sandwiches we'd take with us for the day. I knew that after all my hard work Shadow was good enough, and I felt sure that we should get a place.

To train a dog for competition obedience is a daily dedication. I had learnt a lot over the last few months, both from people who train dogs and Shadow herself. Twice a day we would go out for our training but I'd soon realized that it was pointless doing this in a regimented fashion. Constant repetition would only bore Shadow, and yet constant repetition is needed for a dog to understand exactly what's required of her in each excerise. So it had to be a mixture of work and play. Each exercise had to be made into a game so that Shadow learnt something without realizing she was working. Just like children, dogs learn much quicker if it's fun.

Our first show was held at the Bingley Halls, Stafford. Shadow was entered in the two lowest classes – beginner and novice. Both the beginner and novice classes have the same pattern of work, the only difference being that the retrieve article in beginner's can be anything, in novice it must be a dumb-bell. There was the same set heel work pattern for each competitor, with right, left and about turns, and halts, where Shadow had to sit absolutely straight or she'd lose half a point. She would also lose points if she walked wide. She had to keep by my left leg in a consistent position. The heel work was first done on the lead and then off the lead, which should, of course, make no difference to a correctly trained dog. The dog is expected to do a recall off the lead: the dog is left sitting at one side of the ring, the handler walks to the opposite end, turns to face her dog and only calls the dog when commanded by the steward. The dog must come to her handler at a reasonable pace – some judges will dock for slow returns on recalls – and then sit in front of the handler exactly in the middle of the handler's two feet. An off-centre present or a crooked sit will lose another half a mark. The dog must then return to the heel position by either going right round the handler's back, or turning and sitting at the left hand side. Another half a point is lost if the sit at the heel position isn't absolutely straight.

Retrieve for a beginner handler is one of the hardest exercises to teach a dog. It takes a lot of time and patience to get the required precision. The handler begins the exercise, as always, with the dog sitting on the left, and throws out the retrieve article. The dog must sit and wait until told by the handler to retrieve. If the dog knocks the article with her paws or throws it about at all in her mouth, she will be docked points. So she must do a very clean pick-up, immediately returning to the handler to do a straight sit in front again, hold the article until the handler takes it and then return again to the heel position.

The stays are done with all the dogs that are entered in the class together, usually in a separate ring. The dogs in beginner and novice are left in a one minute sit and then a two minute down, and the handlers are only required to move a few yards away from the dog. It is always a nice feeling just before going in the ring because everyone starts with the maximum amount of points – a hundred for novice and beginner's. For each fault points are knocked off so, naturally, it's the person with the highest number of points who wins the day.

The competition at dog shows nowadays is extremely fierce. There are as many as sixty dogs in each class, so a judge takes from around ten o'clock in the morning until five or six o'clock at night to get through all the entries. With such strong competition for the places, it's often only half a mark lost that can deny you that first place, so you can imagine how much effort and work and enthusiasm must go into the training of your dog to get absolute precision. The classes start with beginners, then go on to novices, A, B and C. Once in A, the dogs are expected to do more complicated exercises! You are not allowed to talk to your dog except to give the commands, and any extra command will be docked from your marks. In the higher classes dogs are expected to do stays while the handlers go out of sight and to discriminate between scent – at first just their owner's scent and then on to someone else's scent. The dogs must work up and down a line of, say, white cloths to scent the correct article. This is something that we humans know nothing about. We can only teach our dogs how to scent discriminate by sight and often when they pick up the wrong cloth we don't know why. They could be air scenting – scent carries on the slightest breeze and scent from one cloth can be blown over to another. One of the most difficult exercises to teach your dog, required for the higher classes, is the send-away. The dog must leave the handler's side and go to a given point that the judge has marked out in the ring and lie down until called back to the handler.

But for the time being, I was just having a try at the lowest classes. As I stood outside the beginners' ring with Shadow sitting at my feet, watching the other competitors, I had never felt so nervous in my life. Television cameras and audiences of six hundred people had never made me so scared as the thought of going into that ring did. I tried not to be nervous for Shadow's sake, for I'm sure emotions pass from owner to dog like radio waves. But, like all good dogs, Shadow knew I was nervous and so put on a very calm front to help me. The steward called my number and I stepped uncertainly into the ring. He didn't seem to notice my shaking hands and trembling legs as he gave me the familiar instructions.

'You can talk to your dog as much as you like but you mustn't touch her. Remember to have a loose lead. You will be penalized if your lead is tight at any time during the exercise. Are you ready?'

I could hardly say yes, my nerves were so bad. I tried desperately to remember all the advice I'd been given: breathe deeply, look straight in front of you, forget about the judge and the steward.

'Dog and handler forward!' the steward commanded.

'Shadow, heel!' I walked round the ring like a jelly, nervous and frightened that I was going to make a mess of it, with little Shadow doing her very best to keep up with my shaky legs and wobbly strides. I was so relieved when we'd done every part of our exercise that I nearly collapsed on the floor with relief.

'That was a nice round,' the judge said. I stared at him, open mouthed. 'You're a bit nervous though, aren't you? You'll have to get over those nerves and your dog will work a lot better. Anyway, you only lost two-and-a-half points. That's very good.'

'Thank you,' I managed to say as I danced out of the ring with Shadow bouncing after me with absolute delight. Two-and-a-half points lost out of one hundred was the best I could ever have hoped for and it gave us reserve place in our class.

I soon realized that before I could go much further up the classes I had to overcome my handicap of sight, or lack of it. However well I trained my dog it was pointless if I was going to walk round the ring in the wrong direction. I certainly wasn't going to give up – never yet had I let my lack of sight beat me, and it wasn't going to stop me showing my dogs. So I had to think of a way round the problem. As soon as I reached any show venue I headed straight for the rings that I would be competing in and sized them up. I walked round and round the outside of them, placing everything I could see in my mind. For example, there might be a tall tree to the left-hand corner of the ring and a yellow car parked on the right. I would then wait and watch the first one or two competitors to see the pattern of the heel work, so I could get it quite clear in my mind that we were doing a right turn towards the yellow car and an about turn towards the big tree. I even admit to going to extreme lengths at some shows, where if I couldn't find any markers whatsoever, I'd have someone stand outside the ring, a little way away, and ask them not to move so that I could pin-point them once in the ring and get my bearings from them. It doesn't always work, but 98 per cent of the time I'm going in roughly the right direction – and if it takes me for the rest of my life, I will master the sport of dog obedience shows.

At our next show, Shadow won first in her beginner class and got a third in the next class. I began to have more confidence in myself and so was able to help her a lot more in the ring. Those first two months of the show season were so enjoyable to both of us. Shadow was placed at almost every show, and the more we worked together, the more the bond of love between us sealed itself. Little did I know how soon it was to end.

Towards the middle of May I noticed that Shadow was limping on her front left leg. For a day or two I thought perhaps she'd strained it, or one of the dogs had pushed her over. When I watched the dogs playing in the park it sometimes horrified me the way they treated each other, racing around at about thirty miles-an-hour, knocking straight into one another. I couldn't find anything wrong with Shadow's paw, or her leg, but after three or four days she was still limping, so I made an appointment to take her to the vet. He was as much at a loss to find anything amiss as I was, and suggested that she could have sprained it and told me to rest her. If there was no improvement I should bring her back in a fortnight. There was no improvement so I took her back. This time I came away with a packet of pills, and instructions to return with her if there was no improvement in a week. I was back at the vet's again a week later. All I remember of that summer is taking Shadow backwards and forwards to the vet. Our fourth visit was for an X-ray. Maybe there was something wrong with her shoulder that would show up. But nothing was revealed on the X-ray and everyone at the surgery was baffled.

Every morning, as I descended the stairs to let the dogs out, I prayed that Shadow's limp would have miraculously disappeared overnight. But although the vet told me he could find nothing wrong with her paw the limp became worse and often Shadow cried out with pain when she lay down or stood up. Back I went to the vet, insisting that this time he do something. More painkillers were prescribed and more X-rays. Poor Shadow was left, yet again, at the vet's surgery for an X-ray and when I called to collect her in the evening, I was met by a pleased grin.

'I've found it!' the vet announced triumphantly. 'She's broken her toe. Often a dog can break a toe, but they usually mend without any trouble at all. Unless, of course, it's a severe break and the dog hasn't been rested,' he explained.

I was personally convinced that Shadow's foot had nothing to do with the agony that she was going through and I told him so, but he insisted that we at least try bandaging her paw and seeing what happened. It was only two days later that I was back, having been told not to return for a fortnight, but the pain was still there. I had never had to deal with a dog in pain before. It was heartbreaking and I felt totally helpless. I faced the vet with determination. 'You have got to do something. It definitely isn't her paw.'

For a moment, I thought he was going to send me home with yet another packet of painkillers and the pain and distress that Shadow was suffering gave me the resolve to tell my vet that he was wrong. 'It's her shoulder that's causing the trouble, not her paw.'

After a moment's hesitation, he suggested yet another X-ray on her shoulder. I wanted to be angry with him and ask him if all his solutions to every problem were X-rays and painkillers, but all I felt was utter despair. So, yet again, I left the surgery without Shadow, with the familiar instruction to pick her up at four o'clock.

At a quarter-to-four I pushed the heavy surgery door open, and walked into the reception area. 'I've come to collect Shadow,' I announced to the receptionist. Not that I needed to tell her. We'd got to know each other rather well over the last few weeks.

'I'm sorry, you can't take her home, they've operated. I'll fetch the vet. Just a moment.'

Relief and foreboding swept over me simultaneously. If they'd operated, they'd found it. Thank goodness! But what was it? The vet grinned at me as he showed me into his consulting room. 'We've found the trouble! There was a lump that showed up on the inside of her shoulder blade so we decided to operate immediately.'

'Yes . . . and what did you find?' I asked anxiously.

'Well, I'm not really sure. Some of the bone there seemed to be dead. I think perhaps she had a foreign body lodged inside but I didn't find anything.'

Together we went through all the things that it might be. A few months earlier, Shadow had a nasty accident with a stick. She'd pounced on it and part of it had stuck in her tonsils at the back. I had to rush her to the vet for an emergency operation to have her tonsils removed. We were lucky that it hadn't punctured her windpipe, but all had been well after the operation. The vet now pointed out that a piece of stick could have been dislodged and gone through Shadow's system and worked its way into some of the bone in her shoulder blade. She could have had a knock or a bite. I couldn't think of any time when that had happened so we decided it had obviously been the stick which had caused the damage.

I went back that day without Shadow but with a much lighter heart and the promise that I could probably pick her up in a day or two. The day or two stretched into ten days. I hate being parted from any of my dogs. This is one of the reasons why Don and I haven't been away on holiday for so many years. There is, surely, no one who would welcome six dogs in a hotel. We have always limited ourselves to day trips to take Kerensa to the seaside or the zoo. It was heartbreaking not to have Shadow at home. The receptionist at the vet showed extreme patience as I rang constantly to ask how

Shadow was and beg for them to let me bring her home. How lucky we are that Kerensa has always been so fit and well and that no illnesses have taken her off into hospital. My sympathy goes out to those poor mothers, for if I was so demented over being parted from one of my dogs, being parted from Kerensa would surely have been unbearable.

'It'll be a long time before she's walking properly again,' the vet warned me. 'Give her lots of rest, and don't let her play with the other dogs.'

At last I returned home with Shadow, armed with pills and instructions, and for a month all was well in our household. Shadow improved daily and began to use her paw again. I had pushed the terror and fear of seeing her in pain behind me and had completely wiped out the thought that I might lose her, until one terrible day when she began to limp again. In my mind I tried to build a wall of resistance, not letting myself think what it could be that Shadow was ailing from. Instead of dwelling on this I went back to the vet to unleash my emotions on him and blame him for her limp. I felt nothing but anger as I stood in the surgery that day, complaining that she was limping again and what was he going to do about it? For a long time he sat at his desk, leafing through the file, not speaking to me, not looking at me.

Well, what *are* you going to do about it? I wanted to yell at him, but something in his manner prevented me. I stood there in silence, watching him. Gradually, painfully, the truth began to seep round my body like ice cold water. I stood there, unable to move or speak, watching the vet leaf slowly through the file.

'I'm sorry, Mrs Hocken,' he began, 'there's nothing more I can do. I think it's bone cancer. But,' he added, 'I'd prefer you to go and see a specialist, just in case.'

I didn't need any encouragement to seek a second opinion, although I knew in my heart that he must be right. I was given an appointment to see a vet at the Royal Veterinary College in Hertfordshire, who specialized in animal orthopaedics. Betty drove the car, as Don was unable to leave his practice. It was a boiling hot August day, something I could well have done without, for I felt sorry for Shadow all the way down, thinking that she was far too hot. But isn't it strange how the memory plays tricks? Although I know there was a blazing sun and azure blue sky, I don't remember it like that at all. I remember it dark, almost black, without colour or sun, but with that terrible heat. Like a tropical night that never ended.

Shadow was taken for an X-ray and a sample of bone was taken from her. I was told I would probably have to wait two hours. I was afraid to ask him then and there whether he could give me the results that day. I didn't really want to know. For two solid hours Betty and I waited. What could I do with myself? I think I talked most of the time. There were pathways and lawns round the big Veterinary College buildings and Betty and I must have walked them a hundred times, while I talked endlessly about anything and everything which didn't concern dogs or vets. I was actually hoarse by the time the vet returned Shadow to me, as much from talking as from terror.

'It'll be about a fortnight before the results are through,' he informed me.

I was horrified. Although I didn't want to know straight away, I couldn't bear the thought of waiting another two weeks. 'Can't you tell me anything now?' I managed to croak.

'Well, I've looked at the X-ray and it doesn't look too promising. We'll ring your vet with the results as soon as we know them.'

A fortnight later, my vet rang me with the worst possible news. I often wonder how vets feel when they have to tell the owners of dogs that there's nothing more they can do and the only advice they can give is to have the dog put down. Of course I know they're not emotionally involved, but I wonder if they ever give any thought to how it will affect the owner. I realize that some owners aren't as attached to their dogs as others. To me, dogs have the same life value as human beings and the responsibility of life or death was laid at my door. I was given a large supply of painkillers for Shadow to prolong her life and to put off my horrible decision.

If prayers and faith and absolute determination could win, then Shadow would have been cured. But they didn't work. All month I put off the decision. A whole month of sleep being the only release from the burden I carried, and each morning when I awoke I prayed that, through some miracle during the night, Shadow would be cured. A verse that I wrote many years ago came into my mind a lot at that point:

> Is hope an indefinite thing
> That comes from a bottomless well,
> Or does it ebb slowly away
> At the beginning of human hell?

I think, at that point, my well was empty. I have often read books in which animals or people die and have shared the grief with the author for many weeks after I've closed the book, but I have never understood the pain and anguish the writer must have gone through to put their feelings into words. And to write is to re-live the whole experience. I am afraid I am unable to share any more of my grief with you, except to tell you that as soon as Shadow began to suffer, she was put to sleep.

CHAPTER SEVENTEEN

I HAVE ALWAYS tried to nurture Kerensa's love for animals, as I realize there must be times when it's difficult to be an only child among so many dogs. And her life, too, must be very different from the children she shares her class at school with. She goes off to dog shows at weekends and her spare time and holidays are often spent walking the dogs. I try to make it interesting for Kerensa by turning our usual dog walks into picnics or training my dogs on a spare field next to the children's play park so that Kerensa can go off and enjoy herself within my sight. It works out very well and I'm sure she gets taken out far more than other children do. I remember when I was her age I would have loved to have had a dog and gone out to dog shows, but times were different then.

I have always loved any animal with fur and four legs, so I've tried to encourage Kerensa to do the same. But I think maybe I've gone a bit too far because Kerensa's love for animals stretches to anything and everything that moves. And things that don't move as well. I have hidden, as much as possible, my fear of creepy crawlies. I didn't want Kerensa to be afraid of them. She was terrified of moths at one point and would scream in the night if a moth flew round her. Although I'm not awfully fond of them either, I feel such things are far more terrifying to a young child. The best way, I decided, was to tell her about moths. So, I invented a family of moths and told her all about them and what they did at home, what they had for tea and the outings they went on, so that every moth that came into the room was one of our six little girls. There was no more screaming in the middle of the night, but there was a bit of shouting.

'Mummy, Mummy, which moth is this? Is it Mary or Miranda or Millie?'

And so it went on, but it worked. It worked beautifully. It worked rather too well for my liking. For Kerensa's desire to know about every living thing that crept became almost an obsession and I had to cover my absolute terror when she walked in the kitchen with caterpillars or worms in her hand. I'd want to run away screaming and tell her to take it away, but instead, I had to put a very brave face on it and explain to Kerensa that creatures like that just had to live outside in the garden, and would she mind taking them back. At the moment we have quite a lot of caterpillars living in our garden because Don has planted some cabbages. Every time he plants cabbages I beg him to spray them, but he never does. So I insist that, if we're going to eat them, he decaterpillarizes them before I go anywhere near the sink that they're in. Kerensa now stands hovering and grabs every caterpillar off Don that she sees, takes it out to her little home for caterpillars, which is actually a dog bowl surrounded by cabbage leaves. Each caterpillar is given a name. The dog bowl is washed out meticulously every day and fresh cabbage leaves are put in. If a caterpillar happens to escape in the night when Kerensa's not watching, all hell breaks loose the next morning.

I wouldn't mind so much if Kerensa's care and attention were only lavished on living things but I'm afraid, at the moment, she doesn't understand what happens when an animal dies. She brought a tadpole back from school. Where she got it from I don't really know, but it appeared from her blazer pocket as soon as she arrived home. Clutching it, she rushed out into the back garden where the stack of dog bowls are kept, filled one with water and, with great pride, placed her dead tadpole in the middle.

'I have called her Julie,' she announced. 'Do you like that?'

'Well . . . yes,' I tried to say without sounding too despondent. 'But the problem is, Kerensa, it's dead.'

'It isn't dead, it's asleep.'

'No, Kerensa, it's not sleeping, it's dead.'

'What do tadpoles eat?' she said, refusing to accept the blatant truth.

That stumped me. I couldn't really think what tadpoles ate. The poor thing stayed in there for days, while I was trying to convice Kerensa that it would never move again. Occasionally she poked it with her finger and whirled the water round, just to convince herself that it was doing something. She'd rush in.

'Mum, Mum, quick, look! It's moving! It's going round and round!'

'Only because you've poked it,' I told her.

'No I didn't. I never touched it.'

After a few days, she wasn't only trying to convince me that it was alive, but herself as well. After a week, I'm pleased to say she lost interest because by that time it was disintegrating.

Visitors to our house need to be given strict instructions about Kerensa's 'things' outside the back door.

'Whatever you do,' I told Harold and Betty, 'don't empty that dog bowl full of cabbage leaves and that bowl of water with the dead tadpole in, or she'll never forgive you.'

Harold and Betty had come down to stay for a day to look after our dogs. We couldn't go on holiday because, of course, we couldn't take Emma with us but there were times, I'm afraid, when a night away from home was absolutely essential and on those occasions I had to get someone in to look after the dogs. I'd been extremely lucky in finding Tracey. Purely by accident we came across each other. Don had met Tracey's father at the local pub and the subject of dogs had cropped up.

'My daughter's crackers on dogs,' John had told Don. 'Can she come and see you? I know she'd like to if I tell her you've got that many. She's at college at the moment studying to be a secretary, but I don't think she fancies the idea. It might get her out of the house a bit if she came down to you,' he said, smiling into his beer.

'Fine,' Don said. 'Send her round.'

And so Tracey came. There aren't many people I could trust with my dogs, especially not to leave them fully in charge, but Tracey is one of them. I knew immediately that she had the same love and respect for animals that I did and, from that day on, she was here at every available moment. Weekends and evenings she'd come and help me exercise, groom and train the dogs until she left college. She was at a loose end. There were no jobs to be had. It dawned on me that I had begun to rely on Tracey more and more as the weeks went by so I did the natural thing and offered her a full-time job. It meant I'd have more time to go out on public engagements and I wouldn't be so tied to exercising the dogs every morning if there were other things to do in the house. It worked out marvellously well. Too well in some respects, for Tracey also got hooked on the obedience show world. So if I wanted to go to a dog show on Saturday and Sunday, it was no good asking Tracey to look after the dogs because she wanted to go as well.

The weekend that Don and I had to go away and stay for a night coincided with one of Tracey's dog shows.

'I will stay,' Tracey offered, 'and look after the dogs if you're really desperate and can't find anyone else.' She looked at me with spaniel-looking eyes. I knew exactly how she felt. Missing a dog show was like the end of the world coming.

'It's all right, Tracey. Don't worry. Harold and Betty have offered to come down and look after the dogs.'

'Oh, thank goodness for that,' she sighed.

I'd written a manuscript full of instructions about feeding – what time, how many handfuls of this and that and how many tablets to put in each bowl – about what time the dogs needed exercising, about checking water bowls and not forgetting to feed the rabbits, and please don't throw the caterpillar or the dead tadpole away. . . .

Betty took one look at my instructions and gave a sigh. 'Do you expect me to read through that lot?' she said. 'It'll take me until you come home tomorrow.'

'Don't worry.' Harold came over with his calm, assured smile. 'I know how to look after animals.'

'Of course you do,' I agreed with him, 'otherwise I wouldn't have asked you to come. But I would be grateful if you'd read all these instructions – just in case.'

With a pat on the back and an affectionate kiss on the cheek, Harold saw me out of the front door and assured me that everything would be well when we returned the next day.

Needless to say, all was well on our return, except for Harold and Betty, who did look a bit peaky.

'Now then, old lad,' Don greeted Harold as we came in the front door. 'You look a bit tired, what's the matter?'

'What's the matter?' Harold exclaimed. 'Why didn't you warn me?'

'Warn you!' I said. 'What's happened? Has one of the dogs bitten you?'

'No, of course they haven't,' Betty said.

'Well, what is it? What's wrong?'

'That b—— tripe,' Harold muttered and cursed under his breath. 'Why didn't you tell me about it? If I ever come to feed these dogs again, don't you leave me tripe. Why can't you feed your dogs on tinned food like any normal person?'

I'd always fed tripe because it was so cheap and the dogs looked well on it. Feeding so many dogs is no small expense, and I had searched around for the cheapest and most nourishing dog food possible and I'd come up with tripe.

'Well, what was wrong with it?' I said, puzzled.

Betty, at that point, burst into hysterical laughter.

'What's the matter?' Harold muttered again. 'The smell, that's what's the matter. It's revolting. I've never seen nor smelt anything so foul in the whole of my life.'

It had never occurred to me that he wouldn't like the smell or the look of the tripe I fed the dogs. Admittedly, it's not very pleasant. It's not the nice, white tripe you buy from the butcher's shop. It's green and mottled and, I must admit, it does smell rather horrible. Indescribably horrible, in fact, but I'm used to it now and it never bothers me. When you've had cats and dogs and babies, nothing bothers you any more. I am so used to smells and things that don't look very nice – and the dogs really do love their tripe.

Betty, who was still trying to control her laughter, began to explain. 'I sent him in to feed the dogs,' she said, 'while I was just putting my feet up and having a cup of tea yesterday afternoon. I told him what each dog wanted before he went in. Well, he hadn't been there two minutes when I heard him shouting and swearing and rushing out into the back yard. I thought something terrible had happened, so I ran out. "Harold, what's the matter," I said. Well, he was being sick all over the back yard. I thought he was ill. Then he told me it was the tripe. He couldn't face it. I'd have to do it. He ran upstairs to the bathroom.'

'And what were the dogs doing all this time?' I said. I know what the dogs are like when dinner's being put out. In fact, I often think that if I happened to slip on the floor into a dog bowl, they'd eat me by mistake.

'Well, they were getting a bit agitated,' Betty told me, 'so I thought I'd better feed them. Didn't think it would worry me,' she said, 'until I went into the dog room and picked the tripe bucket up.'

'Then what happened?' I said.

'I ran into the back yard and was sick.'

'Oh dear, oh dear, poor Betty.'

'Well, that wouldn't have been so bad,' she went on, 'if Harold hadn't decided he was going to clean it all up there and then. The best thing, he said, was the hose. So he gets your hose on the tap. "I'll hose the yard down," he says. "They'll never know what happened." He turned the tap on – full on, mind you,' Betty said, looking at Harold in disgust. 'Didn't put it on properly, did he? It shot off and soaked him from head to foot and you had floods all over the kitchen. I'm glad you didn't come back yesterday afternoon. The air was blue with his language and green with that tripe.'

'Then what?' I asked Betty.

'Well, he retired, muttering, upstairs to the bathroom. I didn't see him for another two hours. Said he was suffering from shock. He left me to do it, didn't he?'

'What happened to the dogs then?' I said. 'You did feed them, didn't you?'

'Oh, I managed it in the end,' Betty said. 'After I'd recovered. You need to get used to that smell,' she said, twitching her nose. 'It takes you a long time before you can accept it.'

'I wish you'd stop talking about it!' Harold said, getting his handkerchief out and mopping his brow. 'It's making me want to heave again.' He clutched at the lounge door as if ready to make a bolt for the bathroom.

'All right, Harold, all right. I promise I won't mention tripe again,' I said.

'No, you better hadn't. Next time, if I come and look after your dogs, will you promise me you'll leave tinned food?'

I promised him faithfully that I would.

CHAPTER EIGHTEEN

I WAS HAVING to travel a fair distance to the nearest Dog Training Club. Not that I minded that at all, but there was a growing need locally for a club in or around Stapleford. Every day in the park I was meeting dog owners with problems, and I am one of those people who can't help getting involved, especially if it's dog problems. I'd spend hours talking to people, trying to help them with their dogs. The main trouble with most new puppy owners was that the puppy wouldn't come back. A lot of this, I am afraid, is actually caused by the owner. When I have a new puppy, the very first thing I do is to take her out to a field or the park and let her off the lead. Of course, I am lucky enough to have other dogs that are older and trained and I know they'll come back to me and a new puppy will follow suit. But a small puppy, especially a Labrador – I can't really speak with great authority on other breeds – will usually cling to the person she knows. I carry tit-bits, usually dog chocolate drops, and keep calling my puppy back to me, then I give a chocolate drop, make a fuss, and off she goes to play again. She has therefore, started right at the beginning knowing that there's a time to be off the lead and to play (and she'll get plenty of time for this) so she won't worry about it. Often, people cause problems by not letting their puppies off the lead because they are afraid that they'll run away. Consequently, when they pluck up enough courage to let the dog off the lead, he does run away. Think of it from the dog's point of view . . . freedom at last! He doesn't want to go back home to be shut in and to have his little garden space. He loves the freedom of the park or the fields and you can't blame him. A dog that's exercised regularly every day and given free run and allowed to play with other dogs is quite happy to come back to his owner and go home, and look forward to the next outing.

As I say, I cannot speak with authority about other breeds. Labradors are very people minded and it's extremely rare that a Labrador puppy will run away. But if you are really worried about your puppy and daren't let him off, then take a long, fine rope or nylon cord and take his lead off, put the nylon cord on, give him as much space as you possibly can. You must keep calling him in and making a fuss and giving him tit-bits, and then letting him go and play again. This is the way, of course, to train your puppy right from the very beginning. I surely don't need to add that wherever you let your puppy off, it must be safe and well away from the main road.

Eventually, I was brought to the decision that a local Dog Training Club was just what we needed, so I began to look for a room. That took me a long time as there weren't many church or Scout halls available which would accept a night for dog training. But after months of searching I was lucky to find a room at the local pub where Don partakes of his beverage (his words, not mine). Having secured the room I then wanted a trainer, but I was soon to discover that not many people were keen on taking a beginners' class and accepting the responsibility of having to be there every week at a certain time. So it looked as if it was going to be me. I wasn't very keen on the idea because I didn't feel that I had enough experience, but I supposed I was better than nothing. At least I could set them on the right lines and give them guidance on how to train their dogs. Tracey offered to come and help me and bring her Yorkshire terrier, Jeannie, so that we would have a small toy dog to demonstrate various exercises on. Training a Labrador and a Yorkshire terrier are totally different things.

My first night was very crowded. Lots of different people came with their different breeds of dog – from a great Dane to a toy poodle. I decided that I would show my pupils, first and foremost, what a well-trained dog should look like and what they were aiming for. Luckily, Tracey had done a bit of

training with Jeannie so I asked her if she would demonstrate. Jeannie loves doing retrieves, recalls and stays, but
heel work is a different matter. Everything went fine up to
the heel work exercise and I asked Tracey if she would mind
showing our pupils that a Yorkshire terrier is quite capable
of walking to heel off the lead. I'm not sure whether Tracey
knew what was going to happen because she seemed a bit
reluctant but, after a little persuasion, she agreed. She took
the lead off Jeannie and gave her the command. Tracey
walked confidently down the hall. Jeannie, on the other
hand, turned tail and dived on the nearest person's lap,
proving to all and sundry that Yorkshire terriers are
definitely lap dogs. I, along with everyone else, burst my
sides laughing and followed with a lecture on training dogs
for heel work.

That evening I'd taken Teak, our German shorthaired
pointer, with me, . . . a very unfortunate decision.

'I will now show you,' I told them, 'how a dog should do
heel work off the lead.' Confidently, I marched into the
middle of the hall, sat Teak at my heel, took her lead off and
gave her the command. I, too, marched confidently down
the hall. For a few yards Teak marched with me and,
suddenly realizing that she was off the lead, turned tail and
dived for the nearest lap. I didn't laugh that time but I
noticed Tracey was having hysterics. Having called my class
to order, I decided to get down to the business of showing
everyone the basics. I soon discovered how different people
and their dogs were. There's that old saying that people
grow to look like their dogs – or is it the other way round?
Yes, some of them did, but others were total opposites and I
could tell, after a moment's training, that an owner had
picked the wrong breed of dog. But how do you tell them that
their beloved pooch definitely is not for them? You don't.
You try to make the best of a bad match. I tried not so much
to run it as general training clubs seem to run their nights –
taking each exercise: heel work, stays, recalls, etc. – but to
find out what problems most people had and to take each
dog and owner individually. It was at this point I realized

136

that not only did I need experience, but danger money as well.

'I can't get my dog to lie down,' a young girl with a large cross-bred German shepherd told me. 'I've tried all the ways it tells you in the book but he won't do it.'

I took hold of her dog's lead and walked him to a space. 'It's quite easy,' I told her. 'First of all, get him into a sit.' Her dog sat down quite easily. 'Take one of his front paws, use a little pressure on his shoulder and he's down.' It was as easy as that.

'Oh, I've tried that,' she said, 'but he always bites me.'

I handed the lead back with alacrity. But, of course, dogs usually only protest, growl or bite their owners when they have no respect for them, when owners spoil them and don't make them do as they're told from being young puppies. It's amazing how often you find that stroppy dogs have stroppy owners, and we had our fair share of them, particularly 'Woolly Jumper'.

This was the nickname given to him by Tracey the moment he stepped in our hall. He had, of course, a woolly jumper on, probably knitted before the First World War. It was massive. It went up to encase his chin and his ears, and reached about half-way down his trouser legs. The sleeves, too, were miles too long and it was an indescribable colour, somewhere between green and grey. There wasn't a lot left of it. Most of it was holes. His hair reminded me of one of those old string mops. It hung down lifelessly into his eyes, around his ears and rested limply on top of his woolly jumper. I think his trousers would be best described as Oxford bags. All in all, he looked a complete down and out and I was just about to throw him out as an unwelcome tramp, when I noticed he had a German shepherd with him. The shepherd launched itself like a wild tiger into the middle of the room, giving banshee howls.

'Major, be quiet!' Woolly Jumper cried. 'Now, that'll do. Now stop it, Major.' Major showed no inclination to stop.

Every dog in the room tried to squeeze itself under a chair, while the owners flattened themselves to the wall in terror. I guided Woolly Jumper to the emptiest part of the hall, told him to sit down and try to keep his dog under reasonable control and, if possible, to mute it.

'Oh, don't worry,' he told me, 'he's already trained. I've only come to get a bit more training in, being as I live just up the road. I've been going to another dog club for two years. He's passed his advanced test there.'

I hesitated to think of the standard the other dog club kept.

Somehow, Tracey and I managed to fight our way through that first evening unscathed, despite Major and Woolly Jumper, who insisted on doing an off the lead recall, although I tried very hard to dissuade him.

'I can assure you he will come to me,' he said with great confidence as he took his dog off the lead and gave him a command to wait that almost shook the foundations of the pub. He marched up to the other end of the room, turned and called his dog in. I've got to admit that Major did go to him, but it was the banshee screams, howls and barks on the way that frightened everybody to death.

'The other dog club you go to, have they not given you any advice about this noise on recalls?'

'Oh, he always does that. It's just him. In fact, my other dog does it as well,' he said proudly.

The thought of him bringing two German shepherds the week after was horrific. 'Do you still train the other dog?' I hastened to ask.

'Oh, no. He's in the car. He's fully trained now.'

At closing time, Woolly Jumper was forcibly dragged through the door and to his car by Major. There was a terrible howling, growling and kerfuffle going on outside and Tracey and I, along with the other trainees, went to the door to see what was happening. There was Woolly Jumper standing with his car door half open, Major behind him snarling and the German shepherd in the car doing the same.

'Get back, you brute! Get back! Now let me in.' The German shepherd in the car had no intention of letting him in.

'What's he going to do now?' I asked Tracey.

'Well, if that was me I'd close the car door and go.'

We all stood watching in fascination as Woolly Jumper tried to push the German shepherd back into the car. It leapt from front to back seat, baring its teeth and snapping every time he put his hand in.

'Now you know where all the holes in that jumper came from,' Tracey giggled.

Eventually, Admiral, as the German shepherd in the car was called, was persuaded to let Woolly Jumper in. He took Major by the scruff of the neck, opened the door and threw him in. There was a terrible fight on the back seat of the car where the two shepherds were locked in combat. Woolly Jumper seized his opportunity, slammed the back door, rushed round to the driving seat and was off before any of us realized what had happened.

Each week I armed myself with things in case of a disaster – disasters being accidents by dogs. I was determined that our hall and the surrounding car park should be left as clean as it was when we found it. So each week I would walk into my training club with buckets, scrubbing brushes, plastic bags and bottles of disinfectant. We never actually did have a dog accident; that is, not until Deirdre came with Ben. Deirdre is very small and petite and I had felt sure when they took Ben as a puppy that he wouldn't grow all that big as Bracken was a little undersized for a Labrador and Buttons by no means oversized. But Ben proved all theories of genetics wrong. Ben is one of my failures as far as puppy breeding goes. He reminds me, now I look at him as an adult dog, as somewhere between a cross doberman and great Dane. He's not in the slightest bit reminiscent of a chocolate Labrador. Not that Deirdre and John mind, but I most certainly do.

Ben was a very willing pupil. He would do anything to please . . . usually in the middle of the floor. Every week my buckets and bags came out for Ben, while I pleaded with Deirdre to take him out on a long walk before she brought him the next time.

'I did,' she said. 'He won't do it till he gets here.'

That piece of floor that Ben took to every week was scrubbed, disinfected and polished so well that you could see it as a clean patch in the hall. It got to be known affectionately as 'Ben's Patch'.

I found I was getting terribly involved with each dog and each owner and I was beginning to worry about them. I'd get in on a Tuesday night and tell Don that I was very worried about the old English sheepdog who kept leaping out and trying to bite people. Or about the great Dane whose owners just could not control him. He had no malice, he just wanted to get there quicker than they did. The biggest problem, I found, was that dogs would behave themselves at the training club. Often I would borrow dogs from people to show them how to handle them and how to train them and, of course, they were then on their best behaviour, but it was at home or in the parks that they were their naughtiest. Much as I tried to tell people and show them how to handle their dogs, once they were out of the training club they both reverted back to their old selves – just like children who behave perfectly in the classroom at school, but are little terrors once they get home.

You can imagine my relief when Janel Johnson, a friend of mine who was handling dogs in the top classes at obedience shows and knew a lot more about training than I did, decided that she would take over and start a local Dog Training Club for both beginners and advanced. It was with great relief I passed everyone over to her capable hands.

CHAPTER NINETEEN

EMMA HAD CELEBRATED her seventeenth birthday, a wonderful age for any dog, but life was taking its toll of her. She had lost her sight and gone deaf, though that didn't worry her at all and she was still able to enjoy pottering about the house and garden and look forward, with Labrador keenness, to her meals. All our young dogs always treated Emma with awe and reverence and left her in peace, except Bracken, of course, who always wanted to be washing her face and escorting her up and down the garden. The visits from our local vet became more frequent and more urgent as the illness that Emma was prone to would take her off her back legs and make her feel very ill. Even on her good days I often had to help her to stand up, rub her back legs and escort her into the garden. I hoped and prayed that her back legs would last her out. It was impossible for me to imagine our lives without Emma; she had always been the centre of everything. We circled our lives and our plans around Emma. We hadn't been on holiday because we knew Emma was too old to enjoy a change and to scamper along the sands as she used to do.

Mentally, I divide my life into two sections – before Emma and with Emma – and the two different lives I led were worlds apart. I often think back to before Emma when my life was totally empty. It was a grey world then, a world without events or future. And often now, when my friends talk about when they were teenagers, and how much they enjoyed going to dances, buying make-up or keeping abreast of the fashions, I only look back with a cold shudder to the days spent struggling to work and back on my own, and the evenings of sitting at home and dreaming of dances and boyfriends by the dozen.

Then Emma. A four-legged miracle who stepped into my life and changed everything. The world suddenly became my oyster and I made the most of it. I went everywhere with Emma. Because of her I met people. Everyone was kind and considerate to a blind person with a guide-dog, and nobody ever complained that Emma would never take me to the end of the bus queue but always directly to the bus stop so that she could be first on the bus and have her choice of seats. They never grumbled when Emma took me into the big stores and pushed her way to the counter to get me served first. She wasn't merely a dog, she was my seeing eyes. She was my best friend. I suppose, subconsciously, in having the other Labradors I was looking for another Emma, but I know I'll never find one. There'd be no dog with such intelligence, such ingenuity and a sense of humour. The relationship between a blind person and a guide-dog is so different from that of a pet dog and its owner. I was never able to force my wishes on Emma, I could only persuade her to do things for me and to ask her if she wouldn't mind. I had learnt, through bitter experience, that Emma was always right.

I remember when the subways in Nottingham had just been completed. It was when I was still at work as a telephonist and every lunchtime we would go out for a walk, either to do some shopping or to take Emma into the park. I had finished doing my shopping and was on my way back to work when Emma suddenly discovered the new subways. She was thrilled and took me down and under the tunnel and up the steps at the other side and stood waiting. Even when you can see, you lose your sense of direction in a tunnel, but it's easy once up the other side as you can just look round and see where you are. I couldn't. I had to keep my sense of direction by listening to the traffic, knowing which side of the road I was on, how many kerbs I'd crossed, the texture of pavements, the smell of shops that we passed. Nearly every shop has its own distinctive smell – paper shops, fish and chip shops, greengrocers, draper shops. Well, I'd lost all that down the tunnel that Emma had taken me, once up the other side, I had to decide which way to go to get back to work.

'Left,' I told Emma, 'we're going back to work.' But Emma wanted to go right. 'No,' I said. 'I'm sure it's left. Go back to work, Emma.' But she still insisted that we go right. In my mind, I could visualize a butcher's shop on our right-hand side and was convinced Emma was trying to persuade me to go into it. 'No, Emma, we'll be late for work. Go left.'

It was a struggle and we had a bit of an argument about it but eventually she gave in and turned left. For ten minutes or so we walked along the pavement and eventually Emma sat down and refused to move any further. I realized that we were inside a big building and, much to my astonishment, after asking a passer-by, I discovered that we were in the Victoria Shopping Centre which was exactly the opposite end of town from where I worked. We should have turned right as Emma had directed in the first place, but she was always so good-natured about my mistakes. I put my hand down to stroke her and apologize. She put her nose into it and I felt her tail brushing my coat. I could just hear her saying, Well, it's not your fault you're stupid, is it? Perhaps you'll listen in future. Now, we'd better hurry up and get back to work, you are going to be late.

In all the years that Emma and I were together, she never ceased to amaze me with her intelligence. I remember going to give a talk one evening, which entailed catching a bus out of Nottingham to a little village where I was to talk to some ladies in the WI at St Mary's Church Hall. As luck would have it, I'd caught an earlier bus so there was no one there to meet me at the bus stop. I decided that, rather than wait, I'd get directions and go under my own steam. I always enjoyed proving that, with Emma, I could get anywhere at any time. So when I heard someone passing, I stopped him and asked if he could give me the directions to St Mary's Church Hall.

'Er, yes, my duck. Now then, you see that big sign on that Esso garage down there? Well you turn left.'

I thought, Oh dear, he doesn't realize I can't see, and I felt too embarrassed to tell him. Never mind, I'll let him tell me and then I'll have to wait for someone else.

'Well, you go left down there and you'll see an off licence, it's bound to have its lights on at this time of night. Well, you turn right down that corner, and you'll see a big notice saying St Mary's Church Hall; you can't miss it, my duck.' He then patted me on the shoulder. 'It's all right, love, I've given your dog the directions of how to get there.' And off he went.

I was open-mouthed with astonishment. I knew Emma was clever, I thought, but that's ridiculous.

Without a moment's hesitation, Emma stood up, trotted down the road, took the first left then right and walked into St Mary's Church Hall. I have no idea how she knew. I'm sure it wasn't from the man's directions. I know Emma was clever, but I'm sure she could never read notices. I think that maybe after many years of giving talks and visiting numerous church halls, she knew where we were going and she could probably smell that damp, musty smell of wood a mile away and just headed for the first collection of ladies that she could find.

I often find I'm smiling to myself when I have a quiet moment. My mind lapses back into the past and memories of Emma flood in. In many ways, she was a very self-contained dog. She disliked being treated like a dog and became mortally offended if strangers came up to her and threw their arms about her and tried to make a fuss. She would back off and huff down her nose in disgust. And she made it quite clear that in our partnership she was definitely the leader. I shall never forget one incident that sticks out clearly in my mind of Emma's determination to be always the boss.

At every kerb, Emma would sit. I would listen for traffic and she looked. It was only if I couldn't hear anything coming I gave her the command to cross the road, and if she still sat there, I knew she could see something. But I had become over-confident and, going home from work in the evenings, we had to cross a lot of very quiet side roads. I had got into the habit of giving Emma the command to go forward and stepping out into the gutter, expecting that

Emma would be in front of me. She didn't like this at all. It was a challenge to her leadership and she decided that she would cure me of it. I was anticipating her. I was going first. I had no right to do that. She was the guide-dog. She must have given very careful thought to her plan, for one evening I was waiting to cross the road and all was quiet. 'Forward,' I told Emma and stepped out immediately. Emma stood up, stepped a few paces in front of me and then backed off quickly and sat down with a jerk on the kerb. It had a wonderful effect on me. I jumped back on to the kerb very smartly. I thought I was probably going to get run over, but nothing came. At every kerb, Emma went through this procedure every time I was stupid enough to step out as I gave her the command. It only took her two or three days to cure me completely of the habit.

I must admit that when I look back and think of the things that Emma did and the kind of dog she was, I find it hard even to convince myself that a dog could have been so intelligent. I realized that as Emma grew older and more prone to her bouts of sickness I would look back to the days when she was young and full of life and we worked so well together. How I longed to turn the clock back – not to be blind again of course, but to have Emma's life over again. A day never passed without my wishing I could wave a magic wand and make her three again.

It was 29th November, a Sunday. I usually look forward to Sundays as it's my lie-in day, but this particular Sunday I was going to be busy. Caroline was staying with us for the weekend and Harold and Betty were due to arrive about half-past nine to spend the day with us. I leapt out of bed and groped around, still with my eyes closed, to find something to wear and went downstairs to let the dogs out and put the kettle on. So far, everything was as it should be on a Sunday morning, everything was normal. I felt for the four teabags to put in the pot, still with my eyes half closed and not really awake. Having made the tea and let the dogs in, I went back upstairs to see if Caroline, Don and Kerensa were awake. Half-way upstairs, Kerensa called to ask if I'd made the tea and I heard Caroline getting out of bed. At that point, everything about Sunday 29th November was still good. I was looking forward to the day, I was looking forward to seeing Harold and Betty again and I'd got a specially large pork joint (Betty's favourite) for dinner. I'd spent Saturday afternoon baking, and I'd made a lemon meringue pie, a fruit cake and a trifle with fresh cream on it. We would spend the day talking about Christmas and planning our New Year's Eve party. Don and I always have a New Year's Eve party and Harold and Betty and Caroline were all planning to come.

Don was yawning and stretching. I looked over towards Emma's bed, but she hadn't stirred. Often she needed help to get out of her bed and had to be carried downstairs. I went over to her and stroked her head.

'Come on, Emma. It's time to get up.' I knew she couldn't hear me but that didn't stop me talking to her. It was a lifetime's instinct. I still wasn't worried – often Emma wasn't keen to wake up. She liked to have a lie-in in the morning and as an old-age pensioner it was her right. I went back downstairs to pour the tea, took them all a cup and went back to Emma. I stroked her again. 'Emma, come on. You are lazy this morning.' She didn't move, not at all. I automatically slid my hand down on to her chest. I could feel her heart beating. I lifted her head gently. There was still no reaction. I was trying to stop the voice in my head that was screaming by telling myself not to panic.

'Will you carry Emma downstairs?' I asked Don, trying to sound as calm as possible, 'while I ring the vet.' I tried not to sound hysterical as I told the vet it was an emergency – Emma – and would he come immediately.

Don laid Emma on a thick blanket in the lounge while I filled a hot-water bottle and found another blanket to cover her up with. This was all done in silence. Caroline came downstairs. She could tell something was wrong.

'What's the matter with you two? Aren't you talking this morning?' She put her head round the lounge door and saw Emma. 'Oh!' Caroline immediately assessed the situation

and realized that what I needed was calmness, not panic.
'Is there anything I can do, Sheila? Do you want me to
put the breakfast on? Are Harold and Betty coming for
breakfast?' She carried on a non-stop conversation to keep
my mind occupied. 'Do you want me to feed the cats for
you?'

'No thanks, Caroline, I'll do that. It'll give me something
to do instead of standing here looking out of the window,
waiting for the vet.'

I walked up and down the garden like a zombie carrying
the empty cat bowls, washing them, refilling them with food.
Probably that's the only morning I've never talked to my
cats. I was at the top of the garden when I heard the vet's car
pull up. I dropped the cats' food and ran back down the
garden to open the front door. I motioned to him to come in,
without actually speaking. He followed me into the lounge
and looked at Emma.

'It looks like the usual problem,' he tried to reassure me.
'I'll give her an injection and if you can get some glucose and
water down her, that will do her good. Ah, I'm glad to see
you've given her a hot-water bottle,' he said, as he dispensed
some tablets into a packet. 'There we are, give her those as
well. If she's no better, ring me. Otherwise, I'll pop in
tomorrow.'

His light and breezy assurance gave me a little hope and I
clung to it like a limpet. Before I had time to lapse into
despair Harold and Betty arrived bringing a breath of warm,
friendly Yorkshire air with them. It was good to have lots of
people round me. It was reassuring. I tried desperately to
keep myself busy instead of just sitting in the lounge looking
at Emma, and hoping. I think I cooked dinner, but I don't
remember. And I certainly don't remember eating it, or
what happened to all the baking I'd done the day before. But
every few minutes I went to see Emma, to make sure that she
was comfortable, to refill her hot-water bottle, to give her
another drink. I stood in the kitchen thinking, The next time
I go into the lounge and touch her she'll wag her tail, she'll
open her eyes. But she didn't. It seemed to me that instead of

moving about as I normally did, I was crawling from room to room, that it was difficult to get everything done. I felt as if there were sacks and sacks of weights on my back and I couldn't get rid of them. As the day went on everyone around me was trying to keep cheerful, trying to keep me occupied, but I felt cut off, sealed in a darkness of my own and everything that was going on around me wasn't real. The only reality was Emma and I.

Harold and Betty took their leave at about four o'clock and, when they'd gone, there seemed nothing else to do. We all sat in the lounge quietly, watching, waiting. Don suddenly got up from his chair and knelt down beside Emma.

'She's gone,' he said.

I didn't believe him. It couldn't be true. I don't know how long I sat on the floor with Emma's head in my hands.

I realize that I'm looking for another Emma in every dog we have. In every chocolate Labrador I meet I look to see if it resembles Emma, but I've never met one yet who does. In my own dogs I watch and hope that they'll do something the same as Emma used to do. Perhaps there is a little of Emma in all of the Labradors I have, but not one of them is a patch on the dog she was. You only ever meet a dog like Emma once in a lifetime and that's if you're really lucky. It's difficult to admit, even to myself, that Emma is no longer here. It's much easier to pretend that she's somewhere around. If I'm in the dining room, then Emma is curled up in the hall fast asleep. If I'm in the hall, then she's in the lounge. It's much easier to accept daily life that way. I know I'm burying my head in the sand, but that's much easier than facing up to the truth.

She enabled me to live as normal a life as any blind person could, and was always eager to do her job for me as guide. As soon as I took her white harness from the peg in the hall, I would hear her dancing by the door with sheer excitement. She loved every moment of her work. From the day I met Emma, on 3rd July 1966, she took hold of my life and changed it completely and utterly. She retired in 1975 at the age of eleven, when my eye operation was successful, and went on to enjoy six years of retirement. I can't bear to think what would have happened to me if I hadn't met Emma, for never has one human being owed so much to a dog.

EPILOGUE

WE ARE ALL still here at Stapleford, not having successfully found our kennels yet, but I know in my heart that we will find them because everything comes to those who wait and I have a very wonderful philosophy on life. I believe everything happens for the best, so I'm sure something would have gone wrong if we'd have been able to take up any of those other residences and the place of our dreams is still waiting, as yet undiscovered by us. My daily life continues and, despite the loss of Shadow and Emma, I am grateful for the fact that I have Bracken, Buttons, Mocha and Teak to love and care for. Of course, no one will ever replace Emma but I know there'll be dogs to love in the future and I have the consolation of knowing that the little chocolate Labrador puppy from Buttons and Bracken successfully completed her training and is now guiding a blind person. It's a very heart-warming feeling to know that somewhere there's another little Emma.